THE PRAYING CHRIST

THE
PRAYING CHRIST

A STUDY OF JESUS' DOCTRINE AND PRACTICE OF PRAYER

JAMES G. S. S. THOMSON
M.A., B.D., B.A. (OXON.), PH.D.

REGENT COLLEGE
REPRINT

THE PRAYING CHRIST
Copyright © 1959 by Wm. B. Eerdmans Publishing Co.

Original edition published 1959,
by Wm. B. Eerdmans Publishing Co.
(LCCN 58-59780)

This edition published with permission
by Regent College Bookstore,
5800 University Boulevard, Vancouver, B.C.   V6T 2E4 Canada

First printing 1995

Printed in Canada

Library of Congress Cataloguing in Publication Data

Thomson, James G.S.S.
   The Praying Christ: A study of Jesus' doctrine and practice of
       prayer / James G. S. S. Thomson

       155 p.   22 cm.

   1. Jesus Christ – Prayers   2. Prayers   I. Title

BV229.C63 T384   1995

ISBN 1-57383-049-6

DEDICATED

in affection and gratitude

TO MY WIFE

CONTENTS

PREFACE

Long ago the writer of Ecclesiastes remarked, "Of making of many books there is no end." The observation is particularly applicable to books on prayer. There may, however, be room for yet another contribution to the already vast literature on Christian prayer. In the following pages there is offered a study of Jesus' doctrine and practice of prayer. The book has been written not for the scholar but for the Christian minister and layman.

The Lord's teaching on prayer, and His habits of prayer, are covered in the first two chapters. In Chapter 3 one of Jesus' prayers is analyzed in order to find out what His preoccupations and prayers and concerns were when he communed with the Father. In Chapter 4 Christ's answer to a disciple's request, "Lord teach us to pray," is examined in order to have guidance for our own prayers. Our Lord's present High-Priestly ministry i glory, and its practical implications for Christians today, are dealt with in Chapter 5. In the final chapter the significance of the foregoing for our own prayers is clarified by a study of the Old Testament phrase, "Wait on the Lord."

The writer is under a very heavy debt to many authorities. Those upon whom he has leaned heaviest will be found at the back of the book. These works are listed according to their special relevance to particular chapters. This will facilitate their use by readers who may wish to consul them personally.

If readers are challenged, humbled, and stimulated by this study of Christ's life of prayer, as the writer himself has been, then this unpretentious book will not have been written in vain.

— J.G.S.S.T.

CHAPTER ONE

THE LORD'S TEACHING ON PRAYER

IT IS TO US the most normal thing in the world to discover that Christ devoted much time to teaching an adequate doctrine of prayer to His disciples. Because of what we know of His doctrine of God and man, it would have been a complete mystery to us if prayer had not loomed large in His teaching. Again, He gave Himself so utterly to prayer that it was inevitable that He should give it a central place in His message. It was necessary also that the Twelve should be instructed in it because of their significance for the Church. After twenty centuries of Christian experience prayer is still supremely important, and we who endeavor sincerely to pray are often acutely aware of our need of instruction in it; how much more the Apostles who were to teach and lead the Church!

The material for a study of the Lord's teaching on prayer is confined to the four Gospels. All are important for this subject but of the four Evangelists Luke is the one who places greatest emphasis on prayer. In addition to the material he uses in common with Matthew and Mark he supplies much that is peculiar to his Gospel, and the main lesson he is concerned to teach is the necessity for the soul's communion with God. He enforces that lesson by portraying Christ as the believer's example in prayer. For instance, he shows how our Lord turned to the Father in prayer at all the great crises of His life — at His baptism, before the call of the Twelve, before Peter's confession, at the Transfiguration, and the Crucifixion. It is also Luke who supplies us with the parables of the Importunate Friend and the Pharisee and the Publican, and with a treatise on prayer which accompanies them. These are used to teach the necessity for confidence and perseverance in prayer. Although Luke was a Gentile he manifests a great appreciation of, and a true insight into, the services and prayers of the Temple in Jerusalem. It is probably significant that he opens and closes his Gospel with references to the Temple, the place of prayer and worship (1:8ff., 24:52f.).

It may not be completely out of place here to point out that

Luke's interest in prayer reappears in the sequel to his Gospel, the Acts of the Apostles. Throughout the whole of that fascinating book prayer is a main preoccupation. As Christ was in prayer when the Spirit descended upon Him (Luke 3:21), so were the Apostles before Pentecost (Acts 1:4, 14; 2:1). The close connection between prayer and the awareness of the Spirit's presence and power is again established in 4:31. Jesus' habit of praying during the crises of His ministry is mirrored in chapter 10 where one of the greatest crises in the Church's history, the opening of her doors to the Gentiles, began in prayer (10:9). As prayer was a habit with Christ so with His Church (4:23f., 12:5, 12). It is Luke who supplies us with the first recorded prayer of the Church (4:24-30). Naturally, prayer was a habit with the Church's leaders. They prayed in the course of their ministry (9:40, 28:8), and in times of difficulty (16:25); and they in turn ever exhorted the leaders of the local congregations to pray without ceasing (20:28, 36; 21:5).

The Lord's teaching on prayer as set forth in the four Gospels deals with three main aspects of Christian prayer: its nature, its aim, and its method.

1. First, then, what did Christ teach concerning the nature of prayer? Christian prayer, He taught, has certain distinctive qualities or characteristics.

(i) Christian prayer should be characterized by *importunity*. This is taught in the parable of the friend who came knocking on a neighbor's door at midnight to borrow three loaves (Luke 11:5-8). Jesus had just given the disciples a form of prayer (vv. 2-4), and in this parable that immediately follows He reminds them that they must learn to importune God in prayer. In the prayer He had given, the Twelve were taught to address God as Father. This would inspire in their hearts the confidence that their Father-God would be able and willing to give what they asked in prayer. Since God was their Father He had their good at heart, and because He was their heavenly Father there was no ground for doubting His ability. They must, therefore, importune Him in prayer. The implication in this parable of the Importunate Neighbor is that we may have to wait for the fulfillment of our prayers, but during the waiting period we are to importune God, knowing we shall receive what we ask in prayer as surely as the Importunate Neighbor received what he asked from his friend.

The analogy is startling, but it does not mean that God grants what we ask in prayer in order to rid Himself of the tedium of our importunity; nor does it mean that prayer is an attempt to wring from a grudging God something that we want very badly. As Archbishop Trench says, "We must not conceive of prayer as an overcoming of God's reluctance, but a laying hold of His highest willingness." The neighbor who was importuned at midnight objected not to parting with the bread but to the inconvenience to which he was put. Once persuaded that there was no peace for him until he acceded to his friend's request he got up and gave him as much as he wanted. The lesson is that prayer is never out of season, never inopportune, but to be effective it must be importunate. It is worthy of notice, however, that the man in the parable importuned his neighbor for the sake of a friend, not on his own behalf.

The exhortation that follows the parable provides another ground for the confidence that God responds to importunate prayer. Matthew's account of the exhortation (7:7-11) presupposes a deferred answer to prayer. This tempts men to doubt its usefulness and to give up praying (vv. 7f); but the answer to this despair is in verses 9-11. The worst of fathers may withhold his child's request but at least he will not mock him; the heavenly Father, on the other hand, whose generosity was emphasized in Matthew 5:45, gives good things (7:11), and only good things (James 1:17), and with great liberality (James 1:5). But the good things are given in response to importunate prayer as the three verbs in the present imperative, *ask, seek, knock,* imply. The ascending scale in the importunity is significant; first the simple request, then the concentrated search as for a lost object, and finally the violent knocking as on a locked door. True, confidence that we shall get what we ask in prayer may sometimes be sinful confidence in our judgment, but the secret is surrender to God's will, and tenacity in prayer. Confidence that the Father will give what we ask, and confidence that what He gives is best, are very different things. This, of course, does not mean that forms of prayer other than petition are not important. They are, and may even take precedence over petition, but if we pray as Jesus taught the Twelve in Matthew 6:9-13 doors will open.

(ii) *Tenacity* should also characterize Christian prayer. Christ taught this in the parable of the widow who pestered the unjust judge until she received redress for the injustices under which she labored (Luke 18:1-8). In the preceding verses Christ had referred to His second Advent (17:26-37); now in the parable of the Unjust Judge He urges watchfulness in prayer in view of that event. Efficacious prayer must be tenacious prayer. Indeed the main lesson in the parable is "that men ought always to pray and not to faint" (v. 1). Persistence in prayer as well as continuity is necessary when the answer is delayed. We must keep on praying tenaciously, a delayed response notwithstanding. The Jews taught that men should pray three times each day, but here our Lord says they should pray "always"; a thought that Origen interprets to mean that the believer's life should be "one great connected prayer"; implying that secular acts become acts of devotion when done for God.

The point in the parable is not that the favor, once granted, is delayed; it is the lapse of time between the request for, and the granting of, the boon that tempts men to think that prayer is a waste of time. The widow, however, continued to come long after her original request had been made, and it was her perpetual coming that plagued the judge and finally moved him to pay attention to her plea. That is the point Jesus emphasized: and if an unjust judge yields at last to the tenacity of a mere widow how much more will the Judge of all the earth respond to the tenacity of His elect who in prayer cry to Him day and night? Delay in answering prayer is a reality, and Christ acknowledges that. The difference between God and the judge is not that God does not delay. He does. The difference is in the reason for the delay.

The argument may be stated thus: if God resembled the judge (which in fact He does not) He would not deny the prayer of faith since the judge granted the widow's request; how much more then will He grant the believer's prayer, He being a heavenly Father! It is to faith sorely tried that the judge seems to resemble God. Long delayed answers to prayer engender doubt, they suggest that God is indifferent, that the idea that Christians are the elect is a delusion. The question then asked is, Why this strange delay since it tends to weaken faith and confirm doubt? If God delays we can be sure that His reasons are not identical with those of the Unjust Judge. If He delays it is in order to develop faith that would otherwise remain static; and also to deepen faith, since it is tenacity in prayer in the face of disappointment that deepens faith. The cause of divine delay is divine love: love for the elect whose faith God desires to strengthen, and love for their enemies whom He desires to bring to repentance. In spite of delay, therefore, faith is convinced that God will finally act to vindicate it. Faith learns to be tenacious in prayer knowing that prayer is finally rewarded, that God is in fact pleading the cause of His elect even when He seems to be indifferent, and that when the moment for divine intervention comes God will intervene without delay. God responds to the prayer of the man who refuses to take "no" for an answer.

(iii) Christian prayer is also characterized by *humility*. Jesus taught this in the parable of the Publican and the Pharisee (Luke 18:10-14). Both men presented prayer in the Temple but only the Publican received a response. His prayer arose out of humility, penitence, and an acute sense of unworthiness. The Pharisee's prayer was not accepted because it was the expression of a proud, self-satisfied heart that labored under the fatal delusion that it could, on the ground of its own merit, win acceptance with God. Humility, not pride in one's attainment, is the right disposition in prayer.

In order to understand the Pharisee we must place him against his Old Testament background. It is a staggering fact that in the multitude of Old Testament legal enactments there is nothing about prayer apart from Deuteronomy 26:1-15. Even there it is not prayer that is emphasized but formulae for worship; formulae which were prescribed by the priest and repeated after him by the worshipper. We have in verses 5-11 a thanksgiving or thank-offering for deliverance from Egypt, the gift of a good land, and a fruitful season; then, in verses 13-14 there is a profession of past obedience. Only in verse 15 can there be said to be prayer or supplication. Now in his so-called prayer the Pharisee in Luke 18 was concerned mainly with his profession of obedience. He was in fact still living in Deuteronomy 26.

His prayer was a profession of obedience, the expression of pride in one's religious attainments. Notice these three points. (a) It was customary for Jews when praying to stand, facing Jerusalem, with the head covered, and eyes downcast; but probably when this Pharisee stood to pray he was adopting a conspicuous pose. (b) His prayer was a prayer with or to himself. In other words, it was not really a prayer. In it he congratulated himself on his spiritual attainments. Feeling the need of nothing, he asked nothing. Conceivably the Pharisee's prayer might be described as a thanksgiving, but the elements of self-congratulation and self-contemplation were too prominent to permit even that description. (c) His prayer was devoid of a sense of sin, hence his feeling of self-superiority. He was superior to the rest of men because of what he avoided, and because of what he had achieved. He feels self-acquitted, therefore, and hints that God is in his debt.

How sharp a contrast the Publican's prayer provides! (a) Humility, which determined his disposition in prayer and the content of his prayer, was its chief characteristic. He was humble toward God, refusing even to lift his eyes to heaven, having no ground for self-congratulation or self-confidence before God. He was humble toward his fellows, hence he stood afar off by himself, considering that the Pharisee was a better man than he. Humility also marked his attitude toward himself. The Pharisee had singled himself out as specially righteous, the Publican as specially sinful, hence he kept on beating upon his breast. (b) His sense of sin is expressed in his describing himself as "the sinner," and well known as such. This was the one fact worthy of mention about himself. The Pharisee had put himself in a special category; so now does the Publican, but how different the class, and how different the reason for his choice. His sin was his chief concern. (c) He was, therefore, conscious of his debt to God, and of his inability to pay it; which compelled him to cry for mercy. Divine grace was his only plea.

It is when prayer is offered in the spirit, and from a disposition of humility, that God accepts, hears, and answers. The Publican, who was despised by men, is now justified by God. Christ, who was able to look into the depths of men's sinful hearts, and into the depth of God's superabounding grace, declares that the Publican went down from the Temple justified rather than the Pharisee who trusted in himself as just (v. 9). He who had a reputation for holiness failed miserably in prayer because his prayer arose from a disposition of pride in his self-attainment; he who had a reputation for sinfulness succeeded in prayer because his prayer arose from a disposition of humility. This parable in Luke 18, then, is really a remarkable advance in spiritual experience and in our knowledge of prayer. In it Christ teaches that under the new covenant of grace profession of ritual righteousness has no longer any place in prayer. The essential of true prayer is self-humiliation, the hall mark of false prayer is self-exaltation.

(iv) *Charity* ought also to characterize Christian prayer. Christ taught this in the parable of the Unmerciful Servant (Matt. 18:21-35). See also Matthew 6:14f., Mark 11:24f., where

Jesus again shows that sincere prayer originates in a forgiving heart. The Jewish rabbis taught that three offences were to be pardoned, but while Peter was twice as liberal as they (Matt. 18:21) his standards differed from theirs only in degree. The Lord's seventy times seven symbolizes the limitless forgiveness of God. There is to be no limit to human forgiveness because there is none to God's forgiveness (v. 22).

The master in the parable of the Unmerciful Servant was graciously pleased to wipe out the colossal debt of ten thousand talents by an act of forgiveness, but when he heard that his servant was bent on exacting the uttermost farthing from someone who owed him a miserable hundred pence he brought the crushing debt of ten thousand talents upon the uncharitable servant's head again. Thus Jesus teaches that the prayer that is received by God is the prayer that is offered by a forgiving spirit, the spirit of man who, having been forgiven the incalculable debt he owed to God, now forgives others their debts to him which are so trifling by comparison. God freely remits our debt but only in response to the cry from a forgiving heart (v. 35). And the forgiveness for which God looks in those who pray to Him must be real. It must be from the heart, not consisting in words only; it must be genuine, unreserved, offered again and again, and times without number, and always because the heart inclines that way.

The fact that divine forgiveness depends upon human forgiveness, however, does not mean that the grace of God is conditioned by our imperfect ethics; but it does mean that prayer is an ethical act of worship. Difficulty in forgiving others indicates an inadequate view of our need of forgiveness from God, and of the nature of the sin that requires God's forgiveness. This moral obligation on our part to forgive is implicit in our having been forgiven by God, and in our praying to God. Christian prayer presupposes charity. Those who pray through Christ must have the Spirit of Christ. They must seek reconciliation with anyone who feels that they have wronged him. They must go further and even remove the sense of injury from the mind. "I will forgive but I won't forget" is anti-Christian. He who prays must be in peace and charity with all men, and must rid himself of the blight of an unforgiving disposition.

(v) Christian prayer should also be characterized by *simplicity*. Jesus emphasizes this in Matthew 6:5f., 23:14, Mark 12:38-40, Luke 20:47, where all parade in prayer is condemned.

In condemning all vain show and pretense in prayer our Lord shows the necessity for simplicity and the childlike spirit in prayer.

There was great necessity for such a precept in His day. During the synagogue services those desiring to be thought devout would stand apart from the congregation to pray by themselves instead of following the public prayers; but they prayed loud enough to be heard by, and to attract the attention of, others. Some would take care to be in a public place when the hour for prayer came around, and would stand in the street for a lengthy period. Our Lord's teaching on prayer shows how far removed was all this parade from genuine prayer.

Another evil against which Jesus' plea for simplicity in prayer would be directed would be the Pharisees' habit of using long prayers in order to get money from unsuspecting widows (Mark 12:38-40, Luke 20:47). They concealed their real motives under a cloak of excessive piety consisting of long prayers, long robes and high titles. The widows assumed that these ecclesiastics were men of prayer and deep piety, and could therefore be trusted; but great would be the condemnation of these men in that it would be commensurate with either the reputation for piety which they had cultivated, or with the hypocritical spirit that stooped to make gain out of a reputation for sanctity. It was against all these theatricals in prayer, which reduced prayer to a system of hours and forms and places and postures, that the Lord directed His plea for simplicity in prayer.

The aim of true prayer is to express in the presence of God the desires of the heart in praise and petition, and inevitably that involves simplicity in prayer. Prayer originates in the heart. In prayer we express the inner feelings of the heart before God, hence the need for privacy in prayer (Matt. 6:6), as well as simplicity. "When thou has shut thy door, pray. . . ." It is only then that we can turn our thoughts inward, enter deeply into our hearts, and hold sacred intercourse with the Father. Public or social prayer is necessary but it is a reality only in the measure in which it is offered by those who are habitual in the observance of private prayer. Prayer in the secret place is proof of the sincerity of prayer in the public place.

The necessity for simplicity in prayer is also underlined in the condemnation of what the AV calls "vain repetitions" (Matt. 6:7). The phrase is a splendid one but it is open to misunderstanding. After all, the pestering of the unjust judge, and of the unfriendly neighbor, and Jesus' repetitions in prayer in Gethsemane, all illustrate the need to repeat petitions in prayer. Words may be repeated to express urgent entreaty, sincerity, and earnestness.   No, what our Lord condemns in Matthew 6:7 is the futile practice in which the priests of Baal indulged in I Kings 18:26, when they "called on the name of Baal from morning even until noon, saying, O Baal, hear us."   The Pharisees also used vain repetitions (Mark 12:40, Luke 20:47); a practice encouraged by the rabbinic maxim, "Everyone that multiplies prayers is heard."   It is "the mechanical repetition of a formula as if it were a magical charm" that is here forbidden by Christ.

He condemned this practice because it implies a wrong conception of God.   It assumes that God requires to be instructed in the needs of His children, and that one can weary Him into granting a request.   By contrast Christ counsels prayers that express requests briefly, simply, and trustfully.   Repetition of these is not forbidden so long as it does not become mechanical, and therefore "vain."   In any case, repetition is uncalled for "because your heavenly Father knoweth."   If it be asked, "Then why pray?" the answer is that we do not receive from God what we do not desire; and if we desire something we shall pray for it.   Things that are worth getting from God are worth asking from God, but since God is a Father who knows our needs and wills to supply them we express these needs in few words and in faith nothing doubting. In Matthew 6:7 Christ forbids not long, frequent, fervent prayers, but the assumption that we can extort from God by importuning Him with what Calvin calls "garrulous loquacity."   We must aim at simplicity in prayer.

(vi) *Intensity* is also of the essence of Christian prayer; cf. Mark 13:33, 14:38, Matthew 26:41, where Jesus urges watchfulness in prayer.   In Mark 13:33, watchful, sleepless vigilance in prayer is commanded because of the uncertainty of the Master's return.   The implication is that if the hour of His return were known His servants would be off their guard, there would be no incentive to intensity in terms of watchfulness in prayer, or to following a way of life worthy of those who daily await their Lord's return.   The Greek word rendered "watch" signifies "keep awake," and refers elsewhere to service as well as to prayer (Heb. 13:17, Eph. 6:18).

Jesus urged intensity in prayer upon the Eleven in Gethsemane. Vigilance in prayer is necessary to steadfastness in loyalty to Christ in times of severe trial.   Watchfulness and prayerfulness enable the Christian to triumph in temptation, especially the temptation that is rooted in personal concupiscence and weakness of the flesh, which enables Satan to gain a foothold in the heart. When we fail in watchfulness in prayer, outward circumstances and inward weaknesses conspire to become occasions for sin. God may test the Christian through outward circumstances, but Satan solicits the Christian through the inner subjective sinful condition of the heart. It was to this that Jesus referred when He spoke of the "flesh and spirit" in Mark 14:38. The Christian must watch and pray intently. True, he has the Spirit and life and nature of God within him, but the frailties of the flesh and his inward evil condition are also with him; he must therefore watch and pray.

Faith is also implicit in watchfulness in prayer. Christ emphasizes this in the sequel to the miracle of the barren fig tree, a passage that demonstrates the power of faith when exercised in prayer. Intensity is paramount even here because the degree of watchfulness and faith in prayer is determined by the intensity and the reality of the prayer life. Through watchfulness and faith exercised in prayer the will harmonizes with God's will, trust in His love and power deepens, and prayer becomes effectual, but inevitably this involves intensity in prayer.

(vii) *Unity* will also characterize Christian prayer (Matt. 18: 19). In the verse immediately preceding, the Lord had just assured the Apostles that the Church's judicial decisions would be ratified in heaven, so long as these decisions arose out of united action by the Church; a similar assurance in verses 19f. concerning the prayers of a united Church is now given. A Christian's prayer is effectual when to it is added the prayer of a fellow Christian, or better still the prayer of the whole congregation. The reason is that Christ the great Advocate is present in every group of praying Christians, and presents their prayers to the Father. It is the Lord's presence in the Church through the Holy Spirit that guarantees to her both the power to legislate and the power to render prayer effectual. Prayer offered by a united group of believers will be inspired by the mind of Christ, which the Spirit interprets to the Church, and can therefore be offered in the name of Christ. Conversely, when the Church ceases to depend upon the Spirit to interpret to her the mind of her Lord her authority is abused, the Spirit is grieved, and prayer is rendered ineffectual.

Jesus' teaching in Matthew 18:19f. demonstrates the moral and spiritual power in the united consent of as few as two minds informed by the Holy Spirit, and dedicated to Christ. If these two minds are in agreement about anything concerning the Kingdom and express that agreement in united prayer, God will respond. When believers meet "in My name," that is to say, not only to worship or confess, but to exercise faith in the name, Christ is in their midst to make their united prayers effectual. Quite clearly, if Christians can unite to present to God a specific petition the likelihood is that the petition has the whole-hearted approval of all and is, therefore, probably a wise and a right one, and in accordance with the Father's will.

(viii) *Expectancy* is also of the essence of true prayer. This is perhaps the most important aspect of Jesus' teaching on the nature of prayer, and the most difficult to explain. Certainly much misunderstanding has arisen over this part of His instruction on the subject.

Clearly, if a prayer is only an experiment, if it has neither faith nor earnestness nor sincerity behind it, the chances are it will not be answered. Indeed it may not be prayer at all. On the other hand, our Lord makes this astonishing statement, "All things whatsoever ye pray and ask for, believe that ye receive them, and ye shall have them" (Mark 11:24). But what is meant by faith in this verse? Probably it is not so much the essential for prayer as the element which accompanies prayer, and without which it ceases to be prayer. In the verses preceding Mark 11:24 Christ had caused the barren fig tree to wither, and now to Peter He says that the miracle was due to faith; and Peter is then assured that he, too, may exercise the same power, a power which operates particularly in the sphere of prayer (v. 24). Prayer puts us in touch with the source of power, but it is prayer prompted by faith in God. Jesus' words on this occasion had their miraculous effect because behind them there was faith in the Father. A similar union with the Father is open to the Christian, and the limitless achievements which that union makes possible.

Is every Christian, then, in possession of omnipotence when he prays? The suggestion awakens an uneasy feeling in the mind. Such a facile interpretation is out of touch with the rest of the New Testament teaching on prayer. "Mere" faith does not automatically procure the thing asked for in prayer. Christ added no qualification to the statement in Mark 11:24 but, of course, in other parts of His teaching qualifications were given. Here are a few: to be in the relation with God which ensures this amazing power in prayer, one must be in the right relation with one's fellows (I John 4:20); impossible things become possible to believing prayer only as they serve the Kingdom of God (Matt. 17:18-20); this faith is never detached from prayer, prayer being the sphere in which it must operate if it is to effect deeds of power; this faith is not a once-for-all act, since the Greek tense for the verb in the command, "Have faith in God," means, keep on having faith in God, or keep on having the faith of God, the faith that keeps on relying upon God; this union between faith and prayer implies a trustful attitude toward the Father's grace and omnipotence, therefore the petition in prayer is not the main concern but the Father's will and glory; and finally, the faith that is linked to prayer must be definite in its petition, and must believe that the request has already been granted. When this kind of faith seeks in prayer that which corresponds to God's will (Mark 9:23), unexpected results follow.

So much, then, for Christ's exposition of the nature of prayer. True prayer is in essence importunity, tenacity, humility, charity, simplicity, intensity, unity and expectancy.

2. The second main aspect of Jesus' teaching on prayer concerns its aims. In considering objectives in prayer it is well always to keep in mind that prayer is infinitely more than petition. Even in prayer for others petition is not the sum of the matter. It should include praise for blessings bestowed upon them. Not only so, but petitionary prayer for others is a demanding spiritual exercise. It requires the petitioner to place himself, his means, and his energies at God's disposal for the fulfillment of His purposes for others. Real intercession involves self-dedication. And Christianity being what it is, intercession is an essential part of Christian devotion. Faith in Christ is intercession's motive and dynamic. The man in Christ is no longer an isolated unit but a member of His Body, and must, therefore, learn to pray for others. Now concerning objectives in prayer where *others* are concerned Jesus counsels the Christian to ask for three things.

(i) The exorcising of evil spirit forces from the hearts of those in acute spiritual distress and darkness (Mark 9:14-29). When the Lord descended from the Mount of Transfiguration He was confronted by a demon-possessed lad, out of whom nine of the disciples had been unable to cast forth the evil spirit. When Christ had cast it out He said, in reply to the question put to Him by the nine disciples, "How is it that we could not cast him out?" "This kind can come out by nothing save by prayer and fasting" (v. 29).

In this incident Jesus placed the omnipotence of faith over against the limitation of doubt, and challenged the disciples to believe, and so bring into operation the power of God. The disciples' question, "Why could not we cast him out?" implies that they had attempted to exorcise the spirit, and that they therefore had been hopeful of effecting a cure. We know, too, that they ought to have effected a cure (cf. Mark 3:13-15). Their attempt to do so bespeaks a measure of faith but probably this faith was focused in themselves, not in the power of God; a power of which they were the instruments, and with which prayer, faith, and humility have brought them into touch. Wherein lay the trouble, then? It resided in remissness in prayer since Christ had set no limit to the power of believing prayer (v. 29, and cf. 11:23-24). The breakdown was due not to absence of faith but to prayerlessness. Prayer is the medium through which faith expresses dependence upon the omnipotence of God, and trust in its efficiency.

The disciples' faith exercised apart from prayer was presumption. It originated in self-sufficiency. Had they expressed their faith through the medium of prayer it would have been an acknowledgment that the power to free the lad was of God, and it would have brought that power into action. The Apostles had received grace at the moment of their commission (Mark 3:13-15), but a growing faith and an ever deepening experience of prayer were necessary to maintain them in that grace. It was fatal for the Twelve to assume that the power to heal was in themselves and could be maintained apart from prayer. It is not trust in magical powers that sets free the minds of men, but believing prayer originating in a prepared heart and a disciplined mind. Alas, this unclean spirit in Mark 9 sensed a fatal lack of moral power in the disciples by which alone it could be made to yield, and was therefore able to defy them and dominate the lad. The spirit forces with which the Christian wrestles involve a believing appeal in prayer to the almighty power of God.

(ii) In prayer for others the Lord directs the Christian to give a special place to the mission field. In Matthew 9:35ff. Christ was going "about all the cities and villages" teaching, preaching, and healing, but when He saw the multitudes running hither and thither like a shepherdless flock of distressed sheep the tragic inadequacy of the resources at hand suddenly revealed itself, and pointing to the riches of the harvest, and to the fewness of the harvesters, He urged the Twelve to pray "the Lord of the harvest, that he will send forth laborers into his harvest" (cf. also Luke 10:2).

This is an important principle. When the gospel of Christ has become the power of God unto salvation in a man's life he is dominated by an over-powering concern for others. The need is for men who will proclaim the same gospel to others, and to procure these prayers is essential. It becomes a duty to pray for missionaries and ministers, and as that duty is fulfilled God supplies the need. Probably the Twelve were themselves proof of this since we may well believe that they were the answer to the Son's prayers to the Father for workers; and possibly the Seventy were the answer to the Son's prayers and those of the Twelve. It may not be without significance that in Matthew 9 and in Luke 10, the Twelve and the Seventy are reminded that prayer is the answer to the need for workers and to the vastness of the work.

And the situation that faces the Christian Church today throughout the world reminds us that the need for such prayer is always present because the supply of recruits for the ministry and the mission field always falls far short of the demand. It is salutary to notice that the Greek in Luke 10:2 implies that the Lord of the harvest thrusts forth the laborers with urgency, each one to his task at the right moment, and just where the need is greatest. We must see the need of our own day lying open and naked before us just as Christ saw the crying need of His day. We must also realize that we as Christians are the only agents who can meet that need, and must pray to be made so. If Christians prayed sincerely, as the Lord here directs, the Lord of the harvest would have more laborers at His disposal because such prayer would bring them to a realization of their responsibility. Certainly the Saviour's answer to the problem of the inadequacy of numbers was prayer: "Pray ye."

(iii) In prayer for others Jesus directs us to pray for our enemies. The command is repeated twice in Matthew 5:44, "Bless them that curse you . . . and pray for them which despitefully use you, and persecute you" (cf. also Luke 6:28). The Lord's prayers for His enemies (Luke 23:34, I Pet. 2:23) throw light on the meaning of Matthew 5:44, Luke 6:28.

The enemies in mind are those who persecute Christians because of their faith, and are, therefore, those whom it is most difficult to love. No hatred is so bitter as that which is generated by convictions concerning religion. However, the believer is assured of grace to enable him to rejoice in persecution, and so rejoicing he realizes the possibility of loving, and praying for, his persecutors. This injunction to pray for enemies goes far beyond the Old Testament admonition to love our neighbor; and as we love those whom natural impulse prompts us to dislike, love finds its highest expression in prayer. Tolerance is not enough. The Christian is to love his enemies in a positive way. Persecution is to be met with love that expresses itself in prayer, prayer that is an invocation of blessing. Love is the Christian's spiritual dynamic. It manifests itself at the highest ethical level toward his enemies, enables him to work for their welfare, to become a blessing to them, and to pray for them.

This is how to overcome evil with good, and it is the love of God that has been shed abroad in his heart (Rom. 5:5, 8-10) that enables the Christian so to overcome; but prayer is a powerful ally in this work. The reason for this is not far to seek. Acts of love may be repelled by enemies, the friendly word may be scorned by those who hate us, but prayer that enemies may be delivered from the evil that is their curse is a ministry that they cannot prevent the Christian from fulfilling; a ministry that is particularly dear to the heart of Him who prayed for His enemies when they were nailing Him to His cross.

But these three objectives in Christian intercession of which Christ makes mention in His teaching — prayer for those in deep spiritual distress and darkness, for missionaries, and for enemies — do not by any means cover the full scope of intercession. The passage of time, the growth of a man's interests, the developing factor in his Christian experience, should suggest ever new avenues of intercession. The scope of intercession will keep pace with the growth of the Church, the diversity of her needs, and the ever-growing complexity of the society in which the Church witnesses.

Concerning aim in prayer the Lord next directs us to pray for certain things *for ourselves*. There are three matters here to which He refers.

(i) For the things that minister to our physical wellbeing (Matt. 6:11, Luke 11:3), the simple necessities of life such as food, shelter, clothing, and health. All things needful for the body are probably included in the general term "bread" in

Matthew 6:11. The point that Luke stresses is the continuity with which the Father supplies us with these essentials, the tense of the Greek in 11:3 implying not the supply of these things this once, or on this particular occasion, but unfailingly, for each recurring day. Matthew, on the other hand, implies the supply of these for "this day." But neither Matthew nor Luke goes beyond the New Testament principle of a day at a time, although each implies prayer for the supply of our needs a day in advance!

Our Father knows that we need food and clothing (Matt. 6:31f.,) but we are to take the trouble to ask for them in prayer. True, Christ warns against anxiety about bodily needs but He urges that such anxiety be turned into a trustful prayer for their supply. Anxiety for temporal needs implies ignorance of God's providential care (Matt. 6:8), but the Christian has a Father in heaven who knows his needs and never forgets them, and it is implicit trust in this Father's love that kills all such anxiety.

We are also to pray for divine protection from the disasters that overtake men oftentimes with startling suddenness. For example, in Matthew 24:20 the Lord enjoins His hearers to pray that the tragedy that was to engulf Palestine should not come upon them in winter, nor upon the Sabbath when they would not feel free to flee from the disaster since that would entail a journey far in excess of the statutory Sabbath day's journey. The disciple is to pray that God's judgments will be tempered with mercy. We recall, too, that Christ answered immediately the prayer of the Twelve for deliverance from drowning in the storm on the lake (Matt. 8:26). Notice that it was not the disciples' urgency in prayer in the storm that the Lord rebuked; it was their lack of faith. They cried to Him, but apparently they were unconvinced that their cry would succeed: such is the power of fear and anxiety. When faith rules the heart, faith may still cry with urgency, but not because of anxious foreboding. Christ still checks the storm, and restores tranquillity in answer to prayer, by an exercise of His sovereign power.

(ii) In prayer for ourselves we are also to ask for deliverance from temptation or testing (Matt. 6:13, Luke 11:4). This is further suggested by our Lord's command to Peter, James, and John to watch and pray lest they enter into temptation (Matt. 26:41, Mark 14:38), a command that was given to all the disciples that same night (Luke 22:40, 46).

In all these references temptation probably has reference both to the sorrows of life and to the direct assaults of Satan, which test and refine the Christian. Temptation may signify the situations in which God places us where we must choose the good or the evil as, for example, in Genesis 22:1; and also Satan's solicitations to do evil by making sin attractive (James 1:13). There is, therefore, no conflict between the petition, "Bring us not into temptation" (Luke 11:4), and the injunction, "Count it all joy . . . when ye fall into manifold temptations" (James 1:2). The former refers to actual temptations whereas the latter concerns the circumstances which may become occasions for stumbling; for example, lack of wisdom (1:5), poverty (1:9), or persecution (2:6f.). When the believer is assured that these circumstances are engineered in the providence of God, he rejoices in them.

But in temptation we are to pray not to be tempted above that we are able (I Cor. 10:13). God delivers the Christian from temptation when he places himself in conscious and prayerful dependence upon Him. On the other hand, the child of God should watch and pray lest he enter into temptation because temptation derives its power from the condition in which it finds him, not from its own inherent power. Temptation can be repelled only by watchfulness in prayer.

(iii) The other request which Christians are to make for themselves in prayer is for the Holy Spirit (Luke 11:13). Parents, though sinful, know how to give the best to their children. They do not give a stone for bread, or a serpent for a fish, or a scorpion for an egg: how much more will the heavenly Father respond in love when one of His children asks for the Holy Spirit in prayer, a blessing so necessary to their growth in grace. This verse may be understood to mean that Christians are enjoined to pray for everything that is conducive and necessary to spiritual progress.

For Luke all of Matthew's "good things" are combined in the Holy Spirit. The Spirit's influence and power are productive of good. The Christian's chief good is to resemble Jesus Christ but it is the Spirit who accomplishes this transformation, as Luke must often have heard from Paul. Not that Luke's use of the title "Holy Spirit" in 11:13, in connection with requests in prayer, is fortuitous. There is in Scripture a strong connection between prayer and the Spirit. The Christian has the Spirit of God in his heart, and it is the Spirit who utters the prayers when the believer prays; having, therefore, this Spirit of adoption he cannot but constantly cry out, "Abba, Father" (Rom. 8:15, Gal. 4:

1-3). How practical, then, is this word in Luke 11:13. Arising as it does out of the parable of the Importunate Neighbor Luke's context suggests that the parable was a warning against stopping to pray when God seems to delay the answer to the prayer for the Holy Spirit, for personal holiness, and growth in grace. Christ urges importunity in such prayer, assuring that the Father will give the Holy Spirit to those who ask.

But in all our thinking about objectives in prayer, either for others or for ourselves, we should realize that the aim of prayer is not to suggest something to God which He has not thought of, nor is it an attempt to get Him to change His mind. True prayer originates in the frame of mind that asks God for something that will be a blessing and not a curse. Prayer is the recognition that we must not forget God, nor live in sinful independence of Him. God is the Source of all our blessings, and the way to recognize and acknowledge this is to pray. Nothing so well expresses our dependence upon God for the things that we, or those for whom we pray, need, as humble, trustful prayer to our Father.

3. The third aspect of our Lord's teaching on prayer concerns method in prayer. There are two important matters here, both of which are new and revolutionary.

(i) The first of these new factors concerning method in prayer is the offering of prayer to Christ Himself. He was the recipient of prayer from those who needed His help when He was on earth: cf., for example, Matthew 8:2, 9:18, 28:9, 17; Luke 24:52; John 9:38, 20:28. It is significant that in these references those who came to Jesus Christ as recipients "worshipped Him." The Greek word denotes an act of reverence on the part of an inferior to a superior, or of one who is asking a great favor. In the fourth Gospel this word is used of the worship of God (4:20-24, 12:20). In 9:38 John again uses it of the reverence of the man born blind toward Christ, whom he now believes to be the Son of God; while in 20:28 he uses it of the worship offered by Thomas to Christ whom he calls "my Lord and my God." This was the attitude of those who came to Jesus beseeching a blessing from Him in prayer.

Now the manner in which Christ dealt with those prayers addressed to Him on earth will throw light on the Christian act of offering prayer to Him today. There are four points to be observed here.

(a) Jesus often insisted on faith in the suppliant. We have already touched on the importance of faith in connection with prayer (see pp. 21f.), but it is worth noting again. "Believe ye that I am able to do this?" or words to that effect, was a question that Christ often put to those who sought a blessing from Him. So today He bids men ask as if they really expected to receive, and in every act of prayer believe that they are already receiving.

(b) Again, our Lord did not always grant immediately the boon asked for, in order to create importunity, and to test faith and character. For example, in Matthew 9:27ff., it was His seeming indifference that evoked the insistent cry and tested the faith of the two blind men. Not till He was in the house did He manifest any interest in their plight; but under this strange treatment their faith grew, as is shown by their insistent appeal, their uninvited entrance into the house, and their unqualified "yea, Lord." Such faith must always gain its objective, as it did on this occasion.

(c) The prayer of James and John in Matthew 20:22, which was addressed to Jesus, serves to remind us of our ignorance in prayer (cf. also Rom. 8:26, James 4:3). Our Lord's use of the word cup, which in Scripture may symbolize good success (Ps. 16:5, 23:5, 73:10), ill-fortune (Ps. 11:6), consolation (Jer. 16:7), divine deliverance (Ps. 11:13), and divine wrath (Jer. 25:15, Ezek. 23:32-34, Isa. 51:17, Zech. 12:2, Rev. 14:10), signified on this occasion the sufferings He was about to experience in His Passion. His Passion is also said to be a baptism of suffering in this passage because the waters of affliction were about to pass over His head and submerge Him. Now when James and John prayed Christ to allow them to sit on His right and His left in the Kingdom, their prayer, and their assertion "we are able," showed they neither understood their request, nor did they have at that moment the capacity to undertake all that their prayer involved. Their prayer indicated that their rightful place was the lowest, not the highest seat. How often our prayers reveal a failure to realize the inseparable connection between the throne and the cross, between glory and suffering. The higher the place the deeper the suffering involved. Prayer addressed to our Lord Jesus Christ must be in the Spirit of, and according to the will of, Christ.

(d) Peter's prayer addressed to Christ to bid him walk to Him on the boisterous waves was granted by the Lord to teach him (and us) that prayer and petition may originate in sinful presumption. Prayer is not the means by which we get from Christ everything we want. It is essentially a moral act. In prayer we ask only those things which can be granted by the Giver of every good and perfect gift. Peter's prayer in Matthew 14:28 reminds us of our own proneness to headstrong boldness in the requests we make in prayer. We are still too inclined to put God to the test by asking for a sign in prayer.

Now all this, we suggest, throws light on the act of addressing prayer to Jesus Christ today. Christians in the New Testament thought it the most natural thing in the world to address prayer to their ascended, glorified Lord after Pentecost. Having proved at first hand Christ's power on earth to answer prayer, what was more natural than to address prayer to the same Lord now that God the Father had "exalted him to be a prince and a Savior"? Christians in the New Testament are those "that call upon [or invoke in prayer] the name of our Lord Jesus Christ" (I Cor. 1:2, and cf. Acts 9:14, 21, 7:59, 22:16). This was equivalent to offering prayer to Him; and this Christians have done since the Ascension.

The act of praying to Christ is, however, not only rooted and grounded in Scripture. It is also implicit in Christian theology. This does not mean that Christ competes with the Father for our worship; nor is prayer to Christ an alternative to prayer to the Father. Jesus Christ is not to be thought of apart from the Father, nor the Father apart from the Son. As Thomas Chalmers used to say, "Apart from Christ I have no hold of God at all." We draw near to the Father through the Son, and the Father draws near to us through the Son. Indeed, the blessed Trinity is involved in Christian prayer. The Spirit teaches us how to pray and what to pray for; that prayer is then offered to the Father; but it is offered through, or in the name of, the Son. That, in a nutshell, is the Christian doctrine of prayer; but the believer also feels it perfectly natural to pray to the Father, to the Son, and to the Holy Spirit, as well as to God the divine Unity.

(ii) The second entirely new factor in our Lord's doctrine of prayer, as that affects method in prayer, is prayer in the name of Christ. The offering of prayer to God the Father through the mediation of God the Son was so completely new that it represented a turning point, a new point of departure, in the history of prayer. The concept of prayer in the name of Christ is indispensable to a true Christian doctrine of prayer because, as has just been pointed out, in Christian faith prayer means praying in the Holy Spirit, through the Son, to the Father. Not that prayer in Christ's name diverts prayer from the Father to the Son; rather it gives new access to the Father.

But what does it mean to pray in the name of, or through, Jesus Christ our Lord? It means to pray to the Father as He has been revealed by the Son. Dr. T. D. Bernard says that prayer "in Jesus' name," or "through Jesus Christ our Lord," is not a mere devotional formula "but a new ground on which the worshipper stands, a new plea for the success of his petitions; and, in fact, a wholly new character to prayer, since it must be brought into unison with the mind of Him in whose name it is presented." To pray in Jesus' name is not simply to tack on to our prayers the formula, "through Jesus Christ our Lord," nor is it the equivalent to having Christ's signature to a blank check that we have filled in, and now ask the Father to honor. An ambassador exercises his authority in the name of his sovereign only because he submits to his sovereign's will, and acts as his sovereign's representative. So to pray in Christ's name is to pray as Christ would pray; and surely He has taught us that the true aim of prayer is complete submission to the Father's will, that He may do His will for us, in us, and through us.

In John 16:23-26 the offering of prayer in the name of Christ is spoken of in the most uncompromising and astonishing way. In verse 23 the Lord says, "If ye shall ask anything of the Father, He will give it you in my name." This amazing word is followed by a reminder in verse 24 that hitherto the Twelve had not yet prayed to the Father in the name of the Son. They had not yet prayed to the Father in the Son's name because such an act of worship presupposes the glorification of the Son. That was not yet realized, but "in that day," the day of the Ascension to the Father's right hand Christ would be glorified, and then the disciples would understand that all the Father's activity toward men, and all men's prayers to God, proceed through the Son and His work. The equality of the Son with the Father would be understood, or at least accepted by them. Then they would do in earnest what Christ urges them to do here. They would ask in His name; and they would prove the truth of Christ's assurance, "Ye shall receive." The Son's return to the Father would secure for the disciples knowledge (v. 23) concerning what they should ask for in prayer, answers to their requests (v. 23), and the joy that such an experience in prayer would occasion them (v. 24). And this would be a continuing experience, as the Greek tense for the verb to ask in verse 24 implies. They would "keep on asking" in His name.

Does this mean, then, that there is no limit to the potentialities of prayer to the Father in the name of the Son? When we compare Scripture with Scripture it becomes clear that it would be wrong to conclude that whatever we ask in Christ's mighty name will be granted. There are at least three qualifications to the wide promise concerning prayer in Jesus' name.

(i) In John 14:13 our Lord says, "Whatsoever ye shall ask in my name, that will I do." But then comes the limitation: "That the Father may be glorified in the Son." That is to say, whatever we ask in prayer in Christ's name will be granted so long as it is something that will bring glory to God; or if by granting it the Father is glorified in the Son. The security against asking things in prayer that would not glorify God is the pleading of Jesus' name in our prayers to the Father.

(ii) The second limitation to the promise concerning prayer in Christ's name is in John 15:7. The latter part of the verse reports Jesus as saying, "Ask whatsoever ye will, and it shall be done unto you." But notice what precedes: "If ye abide in me, and my words abide in you." By Christ's words we are to understand His teachings and commandments. Obedience to these words fits the disciple for fruitbearing (v. 3), but it also exercises a very deep influence upon the disciple's prayer life. The petitions he brings to the Father in Jesus' name will be prompted by the indwelling words of the Savior; and these the Father will grant because they are certain to be in line with His will. Indeed it is the whole harmony and union between the Lord and the believer that ensures prayers and petitions that agree with the mind of the Son and the will of the Father. To abide in Christ, and to have His words abide in us, will make us so increasingly sensitive to His leading, and purpose, and will, that we shall pray only in accordance with that holy will.

(iii) The third limitation to success through prayer in Jesus' name is in John 15:16. The staggering assurance is, "Whatsoever ye shall ask of the Father in my name, he will give it you." But in the very same verse Christ says, "I chose you, and appointed you, that ye should go and bear fruit, and that your fruit should abide." That is to say, it is the Christian who obeys Christ, and who brings forth abiding fruit, who is given whatsoever he asks of the Father in the name of the Son; the reason being that such a Christian is likely to ask only what is consistent with the office and character of the Lord.

The tragedy is that our prayers contain requests which, if granted, would not mean that the Father would be glorified in the Son. And the reason why such requests are made by us in prayer is that we do not abide deeply enough in the Son, the Son's words are not allowed to abide deeply in our hearts, we are not habitually obedient to the Son, we do not consistently bear fruit that abides. These lapses in our abiding in Jesus Christ, and in our obedience to Him, result in our prayers being marred by the same sinful spirit of James and John who prayed for places at the right and the left of Christ's throne (Matt. 20:21, Mark 10:37), and who desired to call down fire from heaven upon the Samaritans who refused hospitality to Christ and the Twelve (Luke 9:51-56); or of Peter who prayed in presumption to be allowed to walk on the water to Jesus (Matt. 14:28). In fact, the prayer of James and John in Matthew 20:21 is the classic example of what Christian prayer is not: "*We* would that thou shouldest do for *us* whatsoever *we* shall ask of thee." What they wanted was something that was selfish, and therefore not glorifying to God. It is when we fail to abide in Christ that we begin to forget what sharing His glory involves. Like James and John we begin to think that it means sitting on a throne; in reality it means drinking a cup. But God answers even the prayer that asks for a place at the Savior's right hand in glory: the answer that comes is in the form of a question. "Can you share the Redeemer's sacrifice?"

The sum, then, of the Lord's teaching on prayer is this: its true center is neither our needs, nor our wills. The true focus of prayer is God, and God's will. The true approach, the true method, is in the name of Jesus Christ. That is to say, we make Christ our way of access to the Father. And we do so, not merely, nor primarily, to ask but to live in harmony with His Spirit, and to obey His will. Whatsoever we ask in prayer, be it things spiritual or things temporal, must be subjected to that blessed will. The aim of prayer is not to make God change His will but to enable us to change our mind and disposition, and thus allow Him to do for us and through us what He cannot do until we are fully yielded to Him.

CHAPTER TWO

THE LORD'S PRACTICE OF PRAYER

THERE ARE TWO observations that may be made by way of introduction. (a) When Jesus Christ lived on earth He did really
pray. That is a fairly obvious thing to say, but it does require
to be said because the chances are that we do not take sufficiently
seriously the fact that Christ *did* pray when He was on earth. In
Chapter 1, our Lord's teaching on prayer was outlined, but that
teaching will remain little more than a dead letter until it really
begins to register on our minds that He taught us how to pray
not in word only but also in act. Christ showed us how to pray
by praying. It was when He was "praying in a certain place"
that one of the Twelve said, "Lord, teach us to pray" (Luke
11:1). It was not His teaching on prayer that evoked the request. The request leaped to the lips when one day the disciples,
with hushed and awed hearts, actually watched the Son of God
at prayer. Looking at Jesus Christ praying they suddenly realized
what prayer was. If *that* was prayer they had not yet started to
pray.

(b) The second introductory observation is this: it requires
to be emphasized again and again that our Lord's prayers were
real prayers; more real and intense than any other prayers that
were ever uttered. The reality of Christ's prayer life has never
been more powerfully expressed than in the words of Hebrews
5:7: "Who in the days of his flesh, having offered up prayers and
supplications with strong crying and tears." It may be true that
the majority of the references to Christ's prayer life concern intercessory prayer, but He did pray for Himself; both in Gethsemane
(Matt. 26:39), and in the course of the High-Priestly Prayer in
the fourth gospel (John 17:1-5). We may well be justified, therefore, in assuming that during those many sleepless nights, spent
far away from the haunts of men, when the Son sought communion with the Father in prayer, He prayed for Himself. There
He would recuperate His strength for the task of redeeming a
fallen world, and would make His task, and His needs on His

human side, the subject of prayer. We should remember that the Son of God found that the best preparation for a long, hard day of demanding work was the entering into fellowship with the Father in prayer, there beholding the Father's glory with no veil between, except the thin veil of His true humanity. The Lord's prayer life, then, was a spiritual reality; His prayers were real prayers.

There are some seventeen references to Christ's active prayer life, and these may be grouped under four heads.

1. His prayers at the great events of His life: (a) His Baptism (Luke 3:21) (b) The choice of the Twelve (Luke 6:12f.); (c) The confession of His Messiahship at Caesarea Philippi (Luke 9:18); (d) The Transfiguration (Luke 9:29); (e) In Gethsemane (Luke 22:39-46); (f) On the cross (Luke 23:46).

2. His prayers in the course of His ministry: (a) Before the great conflict with the ecclesiastical authorities (Luke 5:16); (b) Before giving the "Lord's Prayer" (Luke 11:1); (c) When the Greeks came to Him (John 12:27f.); (d) The retiral after feeding the five thousand (Mark 6:46).

3. His prayers at His miracles: (a) Healing the multitudes (Mark 1:35); (b) Feeding the five thousand (Mark 6:41); (c) Healing a deaf-mute (Mark 7:34); (d) Raising Lazarus (John 11:41).

4. His prayers for others. (a) For the Eleven (John 17:6-19); (b) For the whole Church (John 17:20-26); (c) For those who nailed Him to the cross (Luke 23:34); (d) For Peter (Luke 22:32).

These references remind us of the observation that was made in Chapter 1: that Luke is our main authority for a study of our Lord's prayer life (pp. 11 f.). He alone tells us of seven occasions on which Christ prayed. These are listed in section 1, except (e); and (a) and (b) in section 2. And it is only Luke who tells us that the Lord prayed for Peter; see section 4 (d). As has already been noticed, it is to Luke that we are indebted for the parables of the Importunate Neighbor, the Unrighteous Judge, and the Pharisee and the Publican; all of which were given to enforce important lessons on prayer, and to show what real prayer is. Naturally, then, we shall have recourse to the third Gospel fairly frequently in this chapter.

It is obvious that we cannot hope even to pass in review all of the incidents in the active prayer life of our Lord within the space of one short chapter. However, as one studies these references, a pattern begins to emerge, and we shall review the references to the prayer life of Jesus Christ within the context of that pattern.

1. First, let us notice when Christ went apart to pray. There is, of course, a sense in which it is not accurate to speak of our Lord participating in prayer at different times and on different occasions. The fact of the matter is that when we study the above list of references to Jesus' life of prayer we find that prayer was not simply a part of His life; it was His life. Prayer was a habitual attitude of His mind and heart. Prayer was the atmosphere in which He lived, it was the air that He breathed. So true was this of Christ that the Hebrew of Psalm 109:4, "But I am prayer"; or, "But I am a prayer," was literally true of Him. This was surely the more remarkable when it is recalled how much our Lord crammed into His three brief years of ministry. But although it would be more accurate to say that prayer was our Lord's life, yet He did, at particular times and on particular occasions, turn aside to engage in prayer. There are three matters to notice here.

(i) Our Lord turned aside to pray in the midst of an almost incredibly busy life, and while subjected to a constantly high pressure of work and ministry. Preaching, teaching, casting out demons, healing individuals or large groups of people, and always surrounded by excited, jostling, seething multitudes whose pathetic eagerness to see and hear must ever have moved Jesus Christ to pity — all this demanding service, all this eager self-giving, was carried on in the atmosphere of prayer. No matter how busy He was, so steeped in prayer was His spirit that He could immediately, and without prolonged preparation of heart, turn aside for long seasons of prayer.

Indeed, our Lord insisted on these extended times of prayer. For example, we read in Luke 6:12 that "He went out into the mountain to pray, and he continued all night in prayer to God." Again, Mark 1:35 informs us that "in the morning, a great while before day [the morning of a day of incredible toil], he rose up and went out, and departed into a desert place, and there prayed." On this occasion it was still dark, and the place He chose was not only isolated, it was "desert," and therefore likely to be avoided by men. Both the time and the place were ideal for an extended period of uninterrupted communion. The Greek tense also suggests this. When the Lord "rose up and went out" that was a once-and-for-all event; but the phrase, "and there prayed, should be rendered, "and there he was praying"; meaning that when the disciples at last found Him He was doing something that had been going on for a long time before they came upon Him.

To spend a whole night, or the greater part of the night, in prayer was Jesus' way of preparing Himself for preaching (Mark 1:35, 38), performing miracles (Mark 9:29), and discovering what the Father's will was in moments of important decision (Luke 6:12f.). For what did our Lord pray on such occasions? Curiously enough we are told almost nothing about this. The only exception is His prayer in Gethsemane. But when we reflect that it was before a hard day's ministry, or after such an occasion as the feeding of the five thousand, or in order to escape the rising tide of unhealthy popularity, or to prepare Himself in Gethsemane for His Passion, that Christ turned aside to pray, we can be sure that in communion with the Father He asked for, and received, a fresh touch of power, mental poise, new strength, illumination and guidance. All these and infinitely more our Lord required in the course of His mission, and apparently the only means open to Him by which He found these was communion with the Father.

That this was a habit with Christ is well expressed by Luke when he remarks that "great multitudes came together to hear, and to be healed of their infirmities. But he withdrew himself in the deserts, and prayed" (5:15f.). These withdrawals in the midst of our Lord's busy life were frequent, according to grammatical construction in Luke 5:15f. As C. J. Vaughan, in his book, *The Prayers of Jesus Christ*, points out, all the main words in this passage are in the plural. Not one but many withdrawals, many wildernesses, many prayers. All this high intercourse was going on the whole time. The withdrawals were repeated, the wildernesses were numerous, the prayers were habitual. The contrast between the Master and the multitude in Luke 5:13-16 is unmistakable. While they were milling around, in the grip of an excitement stimulated by Jesus' teaching and miracles, He sought sanctuary and solitude in prayer.

At least part of the significance of this important factor in the life of our Lord begins to emerge when we consider another incident in the gospel record. What, we may ask, was the real meaning of Jesus Christ's ability to calm, in an instant, the tumultuous seas, and the storm-tossed hearts of the Twelve, in the midst of the tempest on the lake? We have not exhausted the significance of that moment when we attribute His miraculous power over nature to His deity. Part of its significance lies in the fact that He emerged from high converse with the Father on the mountain top to march straight into the heart of that raging sea (Matt. 14:23).

A great lesson indeed for all Christian workers. If we would speak the word with power, or exercise the healing, soothing touch, there must be in the background, unseen, our own conscious communion with God. How soon our puny resources are exhausted unless constantly replenished from the reservoirs of God. How mechanical is our work, how ineffectual is our witness, how powerless is our word, unless all is performed in the atmosphere of prayer. The harder Christ's days the longer His prayer times. The busier He was the greater His insistence on the practice of the presence of the Father. Apparently Jesus Christ knew of no substitute for the daily practice of the shut door, the bent knee, the secret communion.

(ii) Our Lord turned aside to pray when, as truly Man, He was subjected, as we are, to the upsurges of deep emotion, especially the emotion of profound sorrow and of great joy. Unfortunately these emotions disturb our life of prayer because they make us men and women of conflicting moods. Not so our Lord. We have hints in the gospel records that the deep emotions that upsurged from His heart were inevitably turned into prayers.

For example, we have a hint of this in Mark 8:11f., where, when the Pharisees asked for a sign, "He sighed deeply in his spirit." This deep sigh or groan was "in spirit"; that is to say, from the depths of Jesus' being, the spiritual part being the highest part of the personality which would be most deeply affected. This was the effect within Him of the Pharisees' desire to test His power to perform a miracle in conditions which would prove that there was or was not collusion between Him and evil powers. An even stronger word for groaning is used in John 11:33, 38. There it seems to signify that strong pressure was put upon Him as He in His spirit restrained His sorrow. The sense is that His spirit chafed at Mary's genuine grief caused by Lazarus' death, at the perfunctory weeping of the professional mourners, perhaps also at the evident lack of faith in His teaching about death (cf. v. 40). Doubtless, pity would also be present in Jesus' groaning in spirit because He was not only acted upon by the grief of the bereaved sisters; He also shared their distress and carried their sorrows.

But those profound emotional experiences were each invariably turned into a prayer. See, for example, Mark 7:33f., where Christ, when a deaf man was brought to Him, "looking up to heaven (he) sighed." The Lord's glance heavenward did much more than remind the deaf man where the power to cure him was to be sought. In the midst of the emotion that stirred His spirit so profoundly Jesus was looking up to heaven in prayer to the Father for assistance (cf. John 11:41). Whereas similar emotions in us produce moods and mental conflicts that make us neglect prayer, the Lord took these very emotions and blended them into a glance and a prayer heavenward.

The same truth is expressed in those moving words in Hebrews 5:7: "In the days of his flesh, having offered up prayers and supplications with strong cryings and tears . . . and having been heard for his godly fear." That profound statement probably has immediate reference to Gethsemane and Olivet; but it may also refer to other strivings of spirit experienced by our Lord. It may be taken as a window which looks into the total life of Jesus Christ. Through that window we can dimly see the agony of soul in the Son of Man when confronted by suffering humanity, and also in the long, still night of retirement, in the desert or on the lonely mountainside, where His anguished soul sent up unutterable sighs to the Father. We, the sport of moods, neglect prayer; when the human emotions invaded the spirit of Christ they only drove Him the more insistently to prayer, to offer up "prayers and supplications, with strong cryings and tears." This was true even in the awful agony of soul and fluctuation of spirit in Gethsemane and on the cross. Even in those dark deeps of the soul His spirit was in undisturbed communion with the Father, still anchored in that one haven of security — prayer. That is a lesson we need constantly to learn. The varying winds of moods and gusts of emotions that blow upon our spirits should not be allowed to disturb our communion with God. They should be made rather to contribute to our fellowship with God, by turning them into strong crying and tears, and prayers and supplications, as did the Son of Man in the days of His flesh.

(iii) The Lord turned aside to pray in the midst of spiritual conflict and death. There are three occasions to notice here.

(a) The first incident is described in John 12:20-28. Certain Greeks came seeking an audience of Christ, saying to Philip, "Sir, we would see Jesus." On hearing of this the Lord began to say, more to Himself, perhaps, than to the Twelve, that the hour of glory had arrived. The moment had come when the grain of wheat must fall into the ground and die, and so bring forth fruit. After challenging those who desired to serve Him to follow Him, He says, "Now is my soul troubled; and what shall I say? Father, save me from this hour. But for this cause came I unto this hour." And then this hour of spiritual conflict, which had driven Him to prayer, issued in triumph: "Father, glorify thy name." And then the voice, "I have both glorified it, and will glorify it again."

How explain these words, and this profoundly significant incident? In the coming of the Greeks there suddenly broke in upon our Lord's inward sight the vision of the Kingdom of God that would embrace all nations. This was "fruit" indeed. But if so, why was Jesus' soul troubled? Because the presence of the Greeks signalized the drawing near of the Father's appointed hour in which the Son would finish the work the Father had given Him to do. The hour for the breaking down of the middle wall of partition between Jew and Gentile (Eph. 2:11-22) had now come, but the Cross alone could make that possible. The Cross alone could open the door to the Gentiles (Acts 10). But what would that involve? The two paradoxes in the passage make that clear. A grain of wheat can realize its life only by dying, a man can find his life only by losing it. The hour, the certainty of which was recognized from the beginning of the ministry (John 2:4), has now come. This passage is an exact analogy to the agony in Gethsemane, which the fourth Gospel does not mention. As in the Synoptics' account of that incident, so John in this one describes how Jesus' soul was "troubled" at the prospect of death; but the Lord on this occasion, as in Gethsemane, submits to the Father's will in asking the Father to glorify His name as the Son passes through the hour of humiliation and death.

Realizing that the hour of glorification meant the hour of Passion, and that the way to fruitfulness was immolation, as illustrated in the grain of wheat whose life cannot germinate unless it submits to death and burial, the Son breaks into prayer. His first word is "Father." To Him He now prays to be saved not from the hour but out of it, meaning that He does not desire to be kept from ever passing through it, but that passing through it the Father may bring Him safely out of it whenever His will has been accomplished. The prayer is in fact a confession of full surrender to the Father's will, as was His prayer in Gethsemane.

And now that Jesus Christ has consecrated Himself afresh to the doing of the Father's will He asks the Father to glorify His own name through His death; and as the Father responded to the Son at the Baptism (Mark 1:11), and the Transfiguration (Mark 9:7), so He responds to the Son on this solemn occasion in John 12. The Father's response was to the Son an assurance that His prayer was answered; an assurance that would strengthen the spirit of Christ as He passed through the hour of agony and death. The Father had been glorifying the Son's name ever since creation; now He will glorify it again in the Son's death, and in all that would flow from it.

There is one other possible explanation, additional to the one just suggested, why Christ's soul was troubled on this occasion. His death on the cross, involving the deepest physical, mental, moral and spiritual agony for Himself, would also eventually involve His disciples in suffering; and thereby they would be entering into the fellowship of His sufferings. The dual principle of living by dying, and finding by losing, would have to be exemplified in those who would follow Him. To choose Christ leads to fruitfulness through death, and to attainment of life by abandoning it; the Cross being a way of life as well as a way of redemption. All who would follow Him would have to live by this principle — to love one's life is to lose it, to hate one's life is to have it. Here was spiritual conflict indeed, not only concerning Himself, but also all who would desire to be His disciples. And was not the Lord's sorrow and trouble of soul in Gethsemane due, in part at least, to the thought that He was bringing the apostles into a situation where they might not be able to endure? And yet they were the nucleus of the Church. That was why, in the midst of His own sorrow of spirit, He urges them to watch and pray, and He Himself prays for them (Luke 22:31f.).

Naturally, then, as all this sorrow described in John 12:20-28 pressed in upon His human spirit, the Son of Man, in the midst of this spiritual conflict, murmured, "Now is my soul troubled, and what shall I say?" Instinctively He betook Himself to prayer. But what should He pray? "Father, save me from this hour"? Perish the thought! "For this cause came I unto this hour." There is only one prayer possible: "Father, glorify thy name." There is true prayer. The ultimate aim of all prayer is this request, "Father, glorify thy name." To reach that point in prayer is to compress all the wishes and longings of every prayer into a single sentence. "Father, glorify thy name." To pray that prayer is to pray every prayer. How natural, then, and how spontaneous the Father's response to the Son's prayer: "I have both glorified it, and will glorify it again."

(b) The second incident is that of Gethsemane; see Luke 22:39-46. It is characteristic of Luke's account of the events in the Garden that it emphasizes the earnestness of Christ's prayers. The point Luke stresses is not their duration (although Jesus must have spent a considerable time in prayer when the first petition was offered, as is suggested by the question in Mark 14:37, "Couldest thou not watch one hour?") but their intensity, the strained effort which offering them involved. In Luke 4:13 the evil one left Christ until a favorable opportunity should present itself; Gethsemane was such a time. Christ's remark in the upper room that the prince of this world cometh (John 14:30), was made real in the Garden when, in the moment of betrayal, He said, "This is your hour, and the power of darkness" (Luke 22:53). And in that hour of darkness the Son of Man was alone, even the inner circle of the disciples having been left behind. The solitariness, the bloody sweat, the earnestness of His prayers, and the Cross standing athwart His path, find a fitting symbol in "this cup."

In trying to understand this even in our Lord's life it is necessary to realize that this was not an isolated or sudden acceptance of the Father's will. "I delight to do thy will" (Ps. 40:8), had been the ruling principle of Christ's whole life. On the other hand, this should not blind us to the fact that because Jesus Christ was truly man, as well as truly God, it was "natural" that He should desire, *if it were possible,* not to experience the anguish that this part of the Father's will might involve. Jesus' prayers in Gethsemane were in fact an appeal to the Father's affection and power. In these prayers the Lord was not for one moment abandoning the work the Father had given Him to do, but He was asking, in effect, if the Cross was really indispensable to the accomplishing of that mission. He was asking if the Father's omnipotence could not find another means of effecting His will; but this "request" did not mean that He was rebelling against that blessed will.

It is necessary to repeat that this "natural" desire in the human heart of Christ not to have to face this part of the Father's will was not due to opposition to that will. His prayer that the cup should pass from Him never for a moment conflicted with His habitual and perfect submission to the Father's will, whatever that will might involve. The Father's will remained supreme;

its accomplishment was His over-riding concern; whatever it might involve He will accept it. The first prayer in Gethsemane was, "My Father, *if it be possible,* let this cup pass away from me: *nevertheless,* not as I will, but as thou wilt." Now what the Father's response to that first prayer was, is apparent from the second and third prayers which the Son offered in the Garden: "My Father, if this cannot pass away [the sense is, if it is not possible, *and it is not*], except I drink it, thy will be done." Whereas in the first prayer Jesus Christ in His humanity desires not to drink the cup, albeit always willing to do so if it be the Father's will that He should, in the second and third prayers He desires to drink the cup, because He now knows that it is the Father's will that He should. This was the Father's appointed means by which He was to be glorified, and He sanctified, or consecrated Himself (John 17:19), to the task.

This sense of tension between the truly human will of the Son Incarnate and the truly divine will of the Father blessed for ever, is the root of the problem for the exegetes of this passage which describes the Gethemane experience through which our Lord passed. If the conviction that the will of the Incarnate Son was standing over against the will of the Father is true then we must conclude that the Son's agony in the Garden was not physical but spiritual and moral. That is to say, it was not the approaching physical death, *per se,* that occasioned the "trouble" in Christ's spirit but rather the realization that because He stood in a unique relation with God and men the approaching death was a sin-bearing death. Jesus' "soul" began to be "exceeding sorrowful" in Gethsemane because the death which He, the sinless One, would die would be a death for the sinful, it would be vicarious in that it would reconcile sinners to God. That really was "this cup" that Christ prayed the Father to allow to pass from Him; not because He was rebelling against the Father's will but because of the possibility that some other means might be found to effect that will. His prayers in Gethsemane point to the fact that Jesus Christ had a human will that was distinct from the Father's will, but always submissive to that will.

Our Lord's experience in the Garden is of profound significance for the study of His doctrine and practice of prayer. Here in Gethsemane He shows, not by word but by act, what real prayer is. Real prayer is absolute self-surrender to, and absolute correspondence with, the mind, the will, the character, of God. And it is good to remind ourselves that on the Lord's part His was not a cold, unfeeling acceptance of the Father's will in prayer. "He began to be exceeding sorrowful"; He began to tremble and faint. Indeed, so powerful was the pressure on His soul that an angel from heaven came to strengthen Him. But prayer with the Father was His true refuge. It was in communion with the Father that He strengthened Himself for the fierce conflict of the Cross that still lay ahead: "And being in an agony he prayed more earnestly; and his sweat became as it were great drops of blood falling down upon the ground" (Luke 22:44).

(c) The third incident is that of the Cross. As our Lord's life ebbed away, and the horror of contact and conflict with sin and death filled His anguished soul, again He found refuge in prayer. "My God, my God, why hast thou forsaken me?" Then that dread cry of dereliction in the darkness was followed by another agonized prayer. Ere death sealed His lips Jesus Christ's last words were a prayer, "Father, into thy hands I commend my spirit" (Luke 23:46). To the last, in spite of the horror of the past hours and of the present moment, our Lord is still in communion with the Father.

His prayers during his Passion show that part of His support had been the Scriptures of the Old Testament. This is true both of His prayers in the Garden and on the Cross. In Gethsemane He had turned to the Psalms. For example, Psalm 42:5f., with its record of present anguish and confident hope, was present to His mind in the Garden (Mark 14:34). And, of course, the word cup is another distinct echo from the Old Testament (cf. Isa. 51:17, Jer. 25:15, 17, Ps. 75:8). And when Christ was on the cross His prayers betray, very fittingly, that Psalm 22 was present to His mind. We have not only the opening words of Psalm 22 in Mark 15:34, but in Luke 23:4 the words of Psalm 31:5 occur, words which the Lord used in the prayer He offered when He committed His spirit to the Father in the moment in which He expired.

So when the sorrow and anguish of some dark spiritual conflict comes upon us, let us remember the Lord who prayed, "O Father, since this cup cannot pass away except I drink it, thy will be done." And when at the last death draws near to us, and strength is ebbing away, and Jordan's cold waters roll at our feet, let us also remember that Jesus Christ the Son of God died praying.

2. The next question we shall raise in this study of our Lord's

prayer life is, What did prayer mean to Him? It appears from the gospel records that prayer meant four things to Christ.

(i) Prayer, for the Lord, was thanksgiving. There are several references which should be noted in this connection. For example, when the Seventy returned exulting in the subjection of the demons to the name of their Lord, Jesus rejoiced in spirit saying, "I thank thee, O Father, Lord of heaven and earth" (Luke 10:21). Characteristically Luke describes Christ's joy on this occasion as being in the Holy Spirit; suggesting that the joy was in the nature of a divine inspiration. It is true that Christ's actions, His emotions, His words, indeed His whole ministry (cf. Luke 4:1, 14, 18), were "in the Spirit." Here it is His joy that is in the Spirit. There is a close verbal parallel to this Lucan passage in Matthew 11:25-27, but the occasion for Jesus' joyous outburst is not identical in the two accounts. In Matthew it comes immediately after the account of misunderstanding and rejection (11:1-24), and is followed by reports of opposition from the Pharisees (12). In such a context Christ's joy strikes the note of certain triumph in the face of apparent failure, and of joyful acquiescence in the Father's will.

Again, just as Jesus was preparing to utter the word of power at the grave of Lazarus, He lifted up His eyes to heaven and said, "Father, I thank thee that thou hast heard me." Then followed the raising of Lazarus. Clearly, before the Lord came to the grave He had already prayed for Lazarus' resurrection; and having received from the Father the assurance that His prayer would be answered, He now publicly thanks Him. This prayer of thanksgiving offered by Christ is remarkable for several reasons. In it He thanks the Father beforehand for the miracle as if He had already performed it: the words, "Thou heardest me" (John 11:41), which refer to His prayer offered four days before (v. 39) for Lazarus' resurrection, are now followed by the remark, "I said it" (v. 42), that is to say, "I said that thou hadst heard my prayer that Lazarus be raised." This prayer of joyous assurance and thanksgiving also bespeaks a confident knowledge of the Father's will; a confidence that was in Christ's mind continually, since He confesses to the Father, "Thou hearest me always" (v. 42). This suggests that the Son's fellowship with the Father in prayer was not intermittent but unceasing. And this prayer of thanksgiving in John 11 was also a public acknowledgment by the Lord that He could do nothing of Himself (John 5:19-27), and that the power He was about to exercise was from above. How amazingly the Son Incarnate depends upon the Father, and how trustingly He took the Father at His word.

Again, before Christ fed the five thousand, He took the loaves; and gave thanks (John 6:11). So also when He fed the four thousand "He gave thanks" (Matt. 15:36). Matthew, with the other Synoptics, uses the word which means to bless, but John's word means to give thanks, or to be thankful. In verse 23 John repeats the word quite deliberately. The Jewish prayer of thanksgiving, "Blessed art thou, Jehovah our God, King of the world, who causest bread to come forth from the earth," was probably the usual grace or thanksgiving before meals. That this prayer of thanksgiving offered by Christ at the feeding of the five thousand played a significant part in the miracle, and was not merely a perfunctory prayer or act of thanksgiving, is suggested by the fact that all four evangelists report that Christ prayed. There is the further fact that a close connection between the miracle and the prayer is established in John 6:23. Notice should also be taken of the pointed reference to the prayer of thanksgiving and the feeding of the four thousand (Matt. 15:36).

The most solemn prayer of thanksgiving, however, was offered when Christ sat down with the Twelve to keep the last Paschal feast. It must have been with profound emotion that the Son of God "took a cup, and gave thanks" (Matt. 26:27). And yet again, in Emmaus, on the evening of the Lord's resurrection "He took the bread and blessed [or gave thanks]; and breaking it He gave" (Luke 24:30); though the blessing here would be simply the usual form of grace before meat.

The main point that emerges from these references to our Lord's prayers of thanksgiving is that whether He was walking in the light or in the shadow, gratitude was an integral part of His life of prayer. It was not only in life's shining hours that thanksgiving leaped to His lips. Indeed, it would seem that it was especially in the darkness that praise poured forth from His heart. It was when He broke bread and poured out the wine, thus signifying the breaking of His body and the spilling of His blood for the bearing away of the sins of the world, that He gave thanks. It was on His way to Gethsemane and to Olivet that He sang a hymn and gave thanks (Mark 14:26). The hymn sung at the moment reported by Mark would be the second part (Ps. 115-118) of the Great Hallel (Ps. 113-118, 136) which the Jews sang at the Passover supper. The second part accompanied the fourth Passover cup, and brought the Paschal meal to a close.

The earlier part of the Hallel was sung at the point in the Pass-over ritual when the lamb was placed on the table. When Christ joined the disciples in singing the Hallel He was, of course, on the way to Calvary.

(ii) Prayer, for our Lord, was also the taking of solemn counsel with the Father. The choice of the Twelve was, for our Lord, a decision fraught with such grave consequences that it was only after spending the preceeding night in prayer that He made the choice (Luke 6:12f.). Luke alone of the four evangelists gives the impression that something of great importance was about to take place. So momentous was the choice of the Twelve that Jesus felt that a long vigil in prayer alone was essential. Luke's phrase is also noteworthy. It is, "prayer to God" (lit. prayer of God), and is used only by Luke, and only on this occasion. It was in this "prayer of God" that Christ "continued all night." Obviously the sense is that in a very special way the Father was the object of the Son's prayers on this occasion, the emphasis being not on the night-long vigil, though that was important, but on the kind of prayer in which Jesus was engaged. It was not merely uninterrupted, but it was characterized by high spiritual intensity; it was the earnest concentration of spirit that was unabated the whole night through. This was not petition but communion, the communion of the Son with the Father whom He worshipped with adoring contemplation.

Now it was during this night-long vigil spent in the highest form of communion possible for the Incarnate Son that He sought and received illumination and guidance concerning the momentous choice of the Twelve. Probably Christ prayed longingly and earnestly over each of the ever-growing number of disciples as He presented them to the Father; and finally there fastened themselves in His mind and heart twelve names. Having had these twelve names communicated to Him in prayer, He went forth in the morning to act upon the Father's guidance. It was through eleven of those men then selected, and later ordained and com-missioned on the evening of the day of the Lord's resurrection, that the world was to hear the Gospel, and receive the faith once for all delivered to the saints. To fulfill such a task they would have to be men who would declare only what their eyes had seen, and their ears had heard; who would not presume on their having chosen Christ as Saviour, but would rely on Christ's choice of them to be His witnesses and disciples. To ensure that the men to be chosen from the now large group of disciples would be of that caliber our Lord found it necessary to take solemn counsel with the Father during a whole night of prayer: "He went out into the mountain to pray; and he continued all night in prayer to God. And when it was day, he called his disciples; and he chose from them twelve, whom also he named apostles."

We would do well to follow the Lord's example in this area of His life of prayer. When we have important decisions to make we too may take counsel with God in prayer, and wait upon Him for guidance. Too often it is dependence upon our own uninformed insight, our own vaunted cleverness, our over-rated ability to weigh up all the factors, that leads us astray. If we took counsel with God more often we would have a greater awareness of the innate tendency to have our eye on how and where our own ends would best be served.

(iii) Prayer, for our Lord, was also intercession. In this connection there is one phrase in particular which should be noticed. It will help us to understand better how prayer meant intercession for Jesus Christ. The phrase is, "for their (or your) sakes." For example, in John 11:15, where the Lord announces the death of Lazarus, He remarks that He was glad for the disciples' sake that He had not been in Bethany to heal their friend, that they might believe. The miracle that was eventually performed was for their sakes in that it strengthened their faith. Watching the emergence of Lazarus from the tomb, they came to a greater faith in Christ. The Greek of verse 15 implies, not that faith was born or implanted at that moment for the first time, but that it grew. Their faith in Jesus was stronger and surer than it had been before He raised Lazarus from the dead. An identical effect resulted from the miracle of turning the water into wine (John 2:11). This increase in the disciples' faith would doubtless enable them to see in Lazarus' resurrection a symbol of the raising of those who were dead spiritually (v. 25f.). The Lord raised Lazarus, not only because of His love for Martha, and Mary, and Lazarus, but also in order to bring the Twelve to see that He was the Resurrection and the Life. There is a sense in which we can say that Jesus performed His miracles for *our* sakes. The same holds true of His teaching given to the disciples; but in a peculiar way it applies to His prayers. He did pray for their sakes, and He still prays for our sakes.

And now, for whom did our Lord pray when He was here on earth? In the next chapter we shall see that in the High-priestly Prayer in John 17 He prayed for the Eleven (vv. 6-19); and then for the whole Church (vv. 20-26). In that solemn hour when the Lord offered His great prayer we were in His thoughts and prayers. But He also prayed for the disciples individually.

For example, He prayed for Peter (Luke 22:31-34): "Simon, Simon, behold, Satan asked to have you, that he might sift you as wheat; but I made supplication for thee that thy faith fail not." Satan's desire was that he should try Peter as he tried Job. The figure of sifting wheat, with the accompanying violent movement of the sieve, symbolizes well the violence of the trial that would come upon Peter and his fellow disciples when Christ had been arrested and separated from them. The winnowing by trial would come upon all the disciples, but the Lord prays specially for Peter, he being the leader, the one to whom they looked to be their spokesman, and who had, in spite of a serious weakness, a special gift of faith, which he afterwards displayed so loyally. Peter's ultimate denial showed how badly he needed this special help from the Lord in prayer. Satan had just entered into Judas, and now he begins to work his evil designs upon Peter. But he had not reckoned with the power and the efficacy of Christ's intercessions for Peter. And it was these intercessions that ultimately demonstrated the fundamental difference between Peter and Judas.

The exact terms of the prayer we do not know, but Christ did pray that Peter's faith should not fail completely, for once and for all (so the Greek of Luke 22:32). He did not pray that Peter should be spared Satan's sifting processes, nor even that he should be kept from falling. Apparently that fall was necessary to show an over-confident disciple what his fundamental weakness was. But Jesus Christ did pray that Peter's grievous fall should not be followed by a hardening of the heart, or by a sorrow that worketh death, or by remorse that would drive him to eternal despair. That Christ's prayers were answered is clear from the sequel to Peter's denial. The proof is seen in the melting grief, the bitter weeping, the frank confession. Peter's experience is the classic illustration of the great Pauline phrase, "By grace are ye saved." How precious the thought that the Lord of glory who prayed so effectively for Peter now prays for us as our High Priest before the throne.

The Lord also prayed for the little children: "And he took them in his arms, and blessed them, laying his hands upon them" (Mark 10:16). Mark is alone in reporting that Jesus "blessed" the children; that is to say, prayed over them. But while Matthew simply has, "laying his hands upon them,"' and Luke, "touched them," both probably mean that He blessed them, because the touch, or the laying on, of Christ's hands symbolized His praying for them, and the imparting of His blessing to them. In communicating blessing to the sick and the suffering He laid His hands upon them; if the hand of Jesus healed the sick, cleansed the leper, and quickened the dead, surely it would impart blessing to the children. So reasoned the mothers, at least, when they brought their children to the Lord "that he should lay his hands on them, *and pray*" (Matt. 19:13). And in rebuking any who would prevent the children from being brought to Him, He justified the faith of the mothers. It was natural that Jesus should want to fondle, and lay His hand's upon, and pray for, children, since in them is found the spirit that should operate in the citizens of His Kingdom (Matt. 19:14); the spirit of obedience and faith, docility and confidence toward the Father all loving, all wise, all powerful. It is not surprising that the Greek of Mark 10:16 implies that Jesus blessed the children fervently, over and over again, reluctant to let them go.

Finally, the Lord interceded for those who crucified Him: "Father, forgive them, for they know not what they do" (Luke 23:34). This incident is reported only by Luke. Inevitably, it brings to mind Stephen's prayer for those who were putting him to death (Acts 7:59).

For whom did Jesus pray on this occasion? Probably for both the Roman soldiers and the Jews; but especially for the latter, since the Gentile soldiers were simply performing a duty which the Jews, by their determination to have Christ crucified, made compulsory. And in His prayer Jesus would have in mind the Jewish people rather than their rulers. See verse 35, where Luke remarked that the people simply beheld, but their rulers mocked. This prayer for forgiveness was offered by the Lord on behalf of the Jews because they were crucifying Him in ignorance. They did not know what they were doing at that moment, but they were, in fact, signing their spiritual death warrant. Forty years were to pass before history was to show them what they had done at Calvary; forty years in which to repent toward God, and have faith in Jesus Christ. Some did repent and believe the gospel, and to that extent Jesus' prayer on the cross was answered.

In the first of the seven words from the cross our Lord was practicing His precept concerning love for one's enemies, and the duty of praying for them (Luke 6:27f.). It is so hard for us to forgive, so seemingly impossible to forget the injury, so fatally easy to allow bitterness to linger on, deeply rooted in the heart, a bitterness that is ever ready to break out again, even after the lapse of years. But here, our Lord, in the midst of injury, intercedes on behalf of cruel, violent men. How moving to recall that His voice blended with the sound of the tragic hammering as the cruel nails were driven home: "Father, forgive them."

These references to our Lord's intercessory prayers, offered in the days of His flesh, illuminate His present intercessions for us in glory. He is now our Advocate who prays with us and for us. The realization that Jesus Christ is praying for us now comforts us in the midst of earth's sorrows and tribulations, and causes fears and anxieties to subside. But our Lord's intercessions when He was on earth are also a sore rebuke. They rebuke our chronic prayerlessness, and they condemn the selfishness that characterizes the poor prayers that we do offer in such perfunctory fashion. In the light of the constancy, and the faithfulness of His intercessory prayers, what enlargement, both in scope and intensity, is needed in our intercessions.

(iv) Prayer, for our Lord, was primarily and supremely communion. This is especially clear from Luke's account of Christ's Transfiguration (9:28). "And it came to pass . . . that he took with him Peter and John and James, and went up into the mountain *to pray*. And *as he was praying,* the fashion of his countenance was altered, and his raiment became white and dazzling. And behold . . . Moses and Elijah . . . appeared in glory," but the disciples were "heavy with sleep; but when they were fully awake, they saw his glory." There are two points of special significance for us here.

(a) It is significant that on the Mount of Transfiguration our Lord's whole thought was concentrated on His approaching death. The Transfiguration was at once the pledge of His future glory, and the prediction of His Passion. It is not without significance that it came a few days after the great announcement of His approaching sufferings and death at Caesarea Philippi; and what His Baptism was to the whole ministry the Transfiguration was to the closing phases of it. During His communion with the Father on the Mount, Jesus Christ was completely absorbed in His determination to do the Father's will, even unto the death of the cross; and it was while He thus prayed and communed that He was transfigured. This is what those who desire the transfigured life should constantly remember. The transfigured life which results from the prayer life involves not only the solemn hour of high resolve and resolute purpose on the Mount, but also the agony of conflict with the demon-possessed world on the plain, and the bloody sweat of Gethsemane, and the white-hot pain of Calvary.

(b) But the most significant point for us in this wonderful incident is that Christ was transfigured *while He was praying.* Prayer was the cause, the Transfiguration was the effect. Luke has already reported in his Gospel that it was while Jesus was praying after His Baptism that the heavens opened, the Spirit descended upon Him, and the Father witnessed to Him; similarly, it was while He was praying that He was transfigured. Matthew and Mark in their accounts suggest that the Lord took Peter, James, and John with Him in order to be transfigured before them; Luke, on the other hand, in his account suggests that He took them with Him in order to pray with them.

The reason for this is not far to seek. Doubtless a spirit of heaviness and despondency was depressing the inner circle of disciples since Christ had announced His approaching Passion, and apparently this mood of despair could best be combated by prayer. If this despondency could be changed to a resilient faith in Peter, James, and John, then they in turn would communicate their joy and expectancy to the other nine disciples; but such a transformation could best be affected in prayer. Now, it was while the Lord was so engaged that He was transfigured; and it was in the presence of the Transfigured Christ that joy and faith were exchanged for gloom and despair. Luke's use of the Greek preposition *en* implies, not merely that it was while He was at prayer that Jesus was transfigured, but that prayer was the cause of the event. It was when His whole personality was engaged in prayer, and in the adoration and communion and contemplation and holy desire that constituted prayer for Him, that He was illumined from within. And this was an inward illumination that was different in kind, not merely degree, from the glory that shone from the countenances of Moses (Ex. 34:29f., cf. II Cor. 3:4, 13) and Stephen (Acts 6:15). It was an illumination that shone through the thin veil of His flesh *from within.*

But the fact that Luke makes the Transfiguration incidental to our Lord's original purpose — His search for privacy in order to pray — makes the event significant for a study of the Lord's life of communion with the Father. It helps us to understand what prayer meant to Christ. As the Passion drew nearer, prayer would become an ever greater necessity, and an increasingly profounder experience for Him. The lesson here is that the transfigured life is the result of, or is determined by, the prayer life. On the holy ground of Christ's prayer life we learn that only through prayer which is face-to-face communion with God can we receive the grace indispensable for the transfigured life. The grace of God is indispensable for the transformed life because transfiguration involves the Christian in identification with Christ in His sufferings.

> I lay in dust, life's glory dead;
> And from the ground there blossoms, red,
> Life that shall endless be.

Our Lord's experience on the Mount of Transfiguration shows that the divine glory is unveiled, and the divine voice is heard, only after the preparation of prayer that is communion with God. Here it stands revealed that for Jesus Christ prayer was communion. Prayer that is communion is the prayer that goes to God, not for what He gives, but for what He is; and in the prayer that goes to God for Himself alone God comes forth to greet, and to meet with, the seeking heart; "a blessed invasion of God's presence" takes place, and lo, an earthborn son is transfigured with heavenly glory.

3. We shall endeavor to sum up this study of the Lord's practice of prayer by asking three questions.

(i) Why did Jesus Christ have to pray? He was very God of very God, but in His perfect humanity He recognized, and submitted Himself to, the law of dependence upon the Father; and it is at this point that the significance of the Lord's practice of prayer appears. It is the Son's dependence upon the Father that makes plain the reason why the Son had to pray. On His human side Jesus had to pray because, although He was the divine Son of God, He humbled Himself to become a partaker of our flesh and blood, and was thereby "made like unto his brethren." That necessarily involved true dependence upon the Father.

How otherwise explain the Son's declaration, "As the Father taught me, I speak these things. He that sent me is with me; he hath not left me alone. I do always the things that are pleasing to him"? The Eternal Son surrendered Himself to the Father. That involved a humbling of Himself, even to the death of the cross; and inescapably that involved the Son in trustful dependence upon the Father, and therefore Jesus Christ had to have recourse to prayer.

(ii) The second question is, What significance should Christ's prayer life have for us today? The question has really been answered indirectly many times in the course of this, and the previous, chapter, but two additional observations may be made. If Jesus Christ prayed because in His humanity He felt the need to pray, how much more should we determine to become men and women of prayer? Again, the *act* of Christ Himself praying, not simply His doctrine of prayer, demonstrates both the necessity and the privilege of prayer, and illumines the meaning and the purpose of prayer.

There are some seventeen recorded instances of our Lord at prayer in the Gospels. It is not often realized that these references are scattered over the whole field of His public ministry, from the Baptism in the Jordan to the Crucifixion at Calvary. The account of the visit to the Temple in the course of Jesus' boyhood (Luke 2:41ff.) also indicates that prayer was His habit from His earliest days. These undoubted facts mean that the references to Christ's prayer life form a most solemn witness to the reality and necessity of prayer throughout His whole life, and to His conscious dependence upon the Father for all that He required to enable Him to do the Father's will. The words, "Ask and it shall be given you," may safely be assumed to provide us with an insight into His life of prayer, and of His trustful dependence upon the Father. They also reflect His habitual experience of fellowship and communion maintained in the midst of incredible toil, and ceaseless conflict with the spirit forces of darkness. When He urged the disciples, "Ask and it shall be given you," He was speaking out of personal experience.

(iii) The third question is the crux of the matter so far as we are concerned: What will our response be to the challenge of our Lord's prayer life? No one will seriously doubt that it does constitute a challenge to our so-called prayer life. What a contrast between Jesus Christ's whole nights of prayer, His sustained seasons of sacred communion with the Father, on the one hand, and the haste, the coldness, the thoughtlessness, the selfishness that characterize our prayers, on the other.

We cannot evade this serious challenge by saying that our Lord's prayer life was unreal and, therefore, unmeaningful. At the beginning of this chapter we noted that reality was the hallmark of our Lord's prayers. Nor can we dismiss this matter by saying that Christ's life of prayer is only some kind of external model upon which we are only allowed to gaze with longing eyes and yearning hearts, and then turn away from, saying, "That is not for us." Christ's words, "I have left you an example that ye should follow," are applicable to His life of prayer. Our sins and failures in prayer must not be allowed to convince us that any attempt to imitate Jesus' example in prayer is a mockery, and doomed from the start.

The same Holy Spirit who indwelt the sinless, but nevertheless real, humanity of Jesus of Nazareth indwells us. When we were saved the Holy Spirit brought us into our Lord's glorious and victorious life of power and love, as into His complete submission to the Father's will. "Paul's Christ is our Christ," therefore Paul's experience of the power of Christ as reflected in his Epistles may be our experience too. There is a path open to us, along which lies the possibility of translating the facts of Christ's prayer life into our own life of prayer. That path Jesus Christ has marked out for us by His living example, as well as by His teaching. By His present intercessions for us, and by His indwelling our hearts by the Holy Spirit, He has placed within our reach a spiritual dynamic that will enable us to walk that path; the path of prayer which we have seen Him walk. This pathway of prayer becomes the pathway of power. Jesus Christ stands upon that very pathway now, inviting us to accompany Him on it. Let us, then, respond with glad obedience and complete abandon to our Lord, as He beckons to each of us, saying, "Follow Me."

CHAPTER THREE

ONE OF OUR LORD'S PRAYERS

THE FIRST THREE Gospels give us no examples of our Lord's prayers apart from those offered in Gethsemane. Happily, the fourth does. What is commonly known as the Lord's Prayer is not, of course, a prayer that was offered by Christ to the Father, but the prayer in John 17 is in very truth one that originated in the mind and heart of the Lord, and was actually offered by Him to the Father. The prayer is, therefore, unique in the New Testament. As already noticed, there are a good many references to the prayer life of our Lord in the Synoptic Gospels but they yield little information on the *content* of Christ's prayers. The Synoptics report the content of the prayers He prayed in Gethsemane, but they give us nothing that can begin to compare with John 17. On the other hand, the fourth Gospel has singularly few references to Jesus' prayer life, but it does lay special emphasis on the content of His prayers (cf. 11:41, 12:27, 17). It is incumbent upon us, therefore, to study this one example of our Lord's prayers to find out how He prayed, what He prayed for, how He expressed Himself in prayer, and what His approach was to the Father in prayer.

The prayer has been felicitously named the High-Priestly Prayer of Jesus Christ, and it is not difficult to see why the Christian Church has felt instinctively that it was as High Priest that He offered it to the Father. Notice the following considerations. It was offered by our Lord when He was about to give Himself a ransom for many, and then assume His Priestly office in glory; and this prayer was the occasion of His consecrating Himself both Priest and sacrificial victim in the approaching sacrifice on the cross. It is because this prayer was a prelude to His Passion that we are justified in using the title, the High-Priestly Prayer.

It calls to mind the ministry of the high priest in Israel on the Day of Atonement. As Israel's high priest would be in prayer for himself, his fellow priests, and the covenant community (cf. Lev. 16:6, 33), so our High Priest was in prayer for Himself, the disciples, and the whole Church. Again, as the Hebrew high priest (Ex. 28:3), and the sacrificial victim (Deut. 15:19), were consecrated or sanctified, and through them the community of Israel was declared clean, so on the night on which He was betrayed our great High Priest consecrated Himself, and through His personal consecration the Church was sanctified (John 17: 19). It is also significant that the language of the Epistle of Priesthood, the Epistle to the Hebrews, and of this High-Priestly prayer, have in common the priestly concepts of cleansing, sanctification, perfection, and priestly ministry in general.

So far as the immediate context of this prayer is concerned, it may be said to arise out of, and complete, the teaching given by Jesus Christ in the upper-room discourses (John 13-16). The phrase "these words" (17:1) may be rendered "these things" (RV; cf. 16:1, 4, 6, 25, 33). If this is accepted, the phrase would refer to the things which the Lord had been teaching the disciples in the preceding discourses. This, of course, would also hold even if the AV phrase were allowed to stand: the sense then would be, "These words [in 13-16] spake Jesus and [then] lifting up his eyes to heaven, he said, Father, the hour is come." The Teacher in the discourses now becomes the High Priest in the prayer that follows. And as He prayed He "lifted up his eyes to heaven." This is the third occasion in the fourth Gospel (cf. 6:3, 11:41) on which this lifting up of the eyes to the Father in prayer is recorded. The act suggests complete confidence in the Father, and complete certainty of final triumph (16:33).

This prayer in John 17 falls into four divisions. (i) The Lord is in prayer before the Father for Himself (vv. 1-5); (ii) the Lord then prays to the Father for the Eleven (vv. 6-19); (iii) then for the whole Church (vv. 20-23). (iv) A fitting epilogue then brings this great prayer to a close (vv. 24-26). In our study of the prayer we shall follow these four convenient and natural divisions.

1. Jesus Christ in prayer before the Father for Himself (vv. 1-5). He had come to earth to give men eternal life, which consists in the knowledge of God (v. 3). Having now completed this mission to the glory of God the Father, He asks to be glorified by the Father. Having glorified the Father by His life He now desires to glorify Him by His death, knowing that beyond death He will receive again from the Father the glory He had with the Father before He laid it aside by humbling Himself.

There is a discernible order in this section of the prayer. It contains but one petition, "Father . . . glorify thy Son" (v. 1), which is repeated in verse 5. Then follow two reasons why the petition is being offered: "That the Son may glorify thee" (v. 1); and, "I glorified thee on the earth, having accomplished the work which thou hast given me to do" (v. 4).

First, then, the petition. It begins with the word "Father." This gracious word occurs no fewer than six times in the course of the prayer. In four instances the simple title "Father" is used (vv. 1, 5, 21, 24); in verse 11 we find the phrase "Holy Father"; and then in verse 25 the title "Righteous Father" occurs. Now, twice in this first petition our Lord addresses God as Father. Not *our* Father, nor *my* Father, but simply Father, the divine name that reveals the mystery of redemption. (Cf. Mark 14:36, where the Son's confidence that the Father hears His prayers again comes to clear expression: "Abba, Father, all things are possible unto thee; remove this cup from me.") This reminds us of the simplicity, the confidence, the holy familiarity which characterized the sacred fellowship between the Father and the Son in the incarnational life of the latter. Even in the agony of death it was the blessed word "Father" that sprang from the heart of our Lord (Luke 23:46).

The phrase "the hour is come" in verse 1 should also be noticed. On three separate occasions we are informed that Christ's hour had not yet come (John 2:4, 7:30, 8:20). Later on, the Lord solemnly announces, "The hour is at hand" (Matt. 26:45); and then finally Christ says, "The hour is come" (Mark 14:41). What was this hour which loomed so large in the mind of Jesus? It was the Passion which was now about to begin. It was that long dark hour into which were compressed the anguish of Gethsemane, the shameful mockery of Pontius Pilate's Judgment Hall, the unspeakable agony of the Crucifixion, and the nameless horror of the descent into Hades. Is it surprising, then, that the Lord prayed in the Garden, "if it were possible, the hour might pass away from him" (Mark 14:35)? And yet it was in this hour of shame and apparent defeat that Jesus Christ was to be glorified (John 12:23f., 32, 34)! This is plain also from 17:1, where "the hour" is the appointed hour for the glorifying of the Son, and from the petition that follows, "Glorify the Son." This can only mean that the phrase "the hour is come," far from being a death knell, was a shout of victory! It was as if Christ had said, "Father, at last the hour for which I have eagerly waited. Now, glorify thy Son!" How deep the mystery that by a divine alchemy the hour of defeat and shame may be transmuted into an hour of victory and glory. How deep also is the mystery that Christians shrink from the fellowship of Christ's sufferings, by which they may be made conformable unto His death.

The words "glorify me" (vv. 1, 5) may be taken to mean, "Take me to be with thyself." Christ, having finished the work the Father gave Him to do, now prays to be translated to glory; but since this glory was to be reached through a sin-bearing death on the cross, as well as by resurrection and ascension, Christ in this petition, as the one and only Mediator, is asking for the glory that was His by right, and for strength not to flinch from all that the entering into that glory would involve. Jesus Christ was glorified when His deity was revealed in His triumph over death, a triumph which was manifested in His resurrection and ascension.

And now come the two reasons why the Lord made this request. The first is, "That the Son also may glorify thee" (v. 1). There are three things to notice here.

(i) The Father's glorifying the Son was not an end in itself. It was a means to a higher end — the glorifying of the Father; and the Son glorified the Father by manifesting the Father's glory, because to reveal God in His holiness and mercy is to glorify God. The glorified Son does not detract from, but contributes to, the Father's glory. Even when every knee shall bow, and every tongue confess, that Jesus Christ is Lord, it will all be "to the glory of God the Father" (Phil. 2:9-11).

(ii) But more specifically, how was the Son to glorify the Father? The answer is in verse 2. The means by which He was to glorify the Father was the power or the authority which the Father had given Him, probably at the Incarnation, since the Greek tense in verse 2 implies a once-and-for-all giving of authority; and the manner in which the Son was to glorify the Father was in His giving "eternal life" to as many as the Father would give Him. But the Son could give eternal life only after being glorified; that is to say, only after fulfilling the Father's will, and completing the Father's mission of bringing life and immortality to light through death and resurrection. It was through His redemptive death that the Son was to give eternal life, and since this was to glorify the Father it follows that it was by His death that He was to bring renown to the Father. That is why the Cross is glory. That was how the Cross became the medium through which the glory of the Godhead shone. The Cross was glory because it revealed the triumph and the perfection of divine love.

(iii) But what is this eternal life that Christ bestows upon men through His death? It is the knowledge of God as the only true God, and as Father (v. 3). And this knowledge is not only intellectual; it is supremely a spiritual apprehension of God. Knowledge here means recognition; and it is in essence eternal life because it is knowledge of God the Father and Christ the Son. In our present existence this knowledge is a matter of faith, but in the world to come it will be vision. In this present world knowledge is the faith that God, the one true God, is Father, and that Jesus Christ is the Son and the Father's sent One. Naturally, this spiritual apprehension stirs the heart to desire a closer fellowship with the Father whom the Son reveals, and a more consistent conformity to the Father's will. As verse 3 implies, this knowledge is fellowship with a Person. It is fellowship with a Person because it is knowledge based upon an experience of the Father's saving and sanctifying power through the mediation of Christ the Son, and through the activity of the indwelling Holy Spirit; and being knowledge of a Person it is dynamic because it is of necessity constantly expanding.

The second reason for the petition "glorify the Son" is in verse 4: "I glorified thee on the earth, having accomplished the work which thou hast given me to do." The words "on the earth" for the moment limit the Son's work to that of revealing the Father to men: a knowledge of which revelation is, in essence, eternal life. This was a work which Jesus Christ accomplished prior to the Cross. The son has accomplished on earth the Father's will and mission perfectly (cf. 18:37, 19:30); and now what is uppermost in His mind is the continuance of that work in glory, because in verse 5 He goes on to ask the Father to glorify Him with the glory that was His before the Incarnation. However, the total work Christ came to do included the Cross; it had, therefore, still to be concluded (cf. the phrase "having accomplished" [v. 4] with the words "it is finished" on the cross). The Cross was not an isolated event; it was the culmination of the work Christ came into the world to perform. That is why the Savior's cry "It is finished" has always been such a wonderful word to sinful men. It speaks peace to them because it announced the sealing of the covenant of grace, and became the sure foundation upon which to rest their salvation.

It has already been noticed that the petition in verse 1 is repeated in verse 5: now that this work is all but completed, "Father, glorify thou me." The words "with thine own self" which follow, mean "in fellowship with thee," and are significant for the doctrine of the deity of Christ. In verse 4 the Son is, in Person, distinct from the Father; here in verse 5 the Father and the Son are one, and co-exist in eternal glory. Having served the Father in complete obedience in His Incarnation the Son now anticipates His return to the Father to exist with Him in glory. In this first petition Jesus Christ is praying for complete restoration to His pre-incarnate glory in which He existed in fellowship with the Father (1:1, 14). If, therefore, the phrase "Father, glorify thou me" signifies "take me to be with thyself" it recalls to the believer's mind the entrance of the earthly high priest into the holy of holies to offer the blood of the lamb for the sins of the people. The recollection is strengthened by the two phrases "with thine own self," and "with thee" (v. 5), which mean "into thine own presence," and "in thy presence." Undoubtedly, then, the language of verse 5 is that of the merciful and faithful High Priest who is about to return to the Father's presence with blood and wounds, the infallible tokens of His victorious death and our redemption.

2. Jesus Christ in prayer before the Father on behalf of the Eleven (vv. 6-19). In this section Christ's prayers for the Apostles do not begin until verse 9. What precedes is an enumeration of the claims the disciples have upon the Father's benevolence (vv. 6-8). These claims are: their election by the Father in grace; their disposition, which is evidence of that electing grace of the Father; their having been given by the Father to Christ, to whom they came by faith (6:37, 39, 44, 46); their reception, through Jesus' teaching, of the revelation of the Father, which had involved a recognition that "all things" that Christ had were from God, that His words were divine, that He Himself was from God, and that His mission was divine. In verses 9 and 10 the needs that will arise as the Apostles fulfill their mission make Christ's intercession for them essential. Then in verses 11 to 16 it is their need of Jesus' assistance during His absence from them that is uppermost. And finally in verses 17 and 19 it is their equipment for the fulfillment of their mission that is the subject of Christ's prayers for them.

The first part of verse 6 marks the transition from the first to the second section of the prayer. Jesus had been thinking about the work the Father had given Him to do, that of making the Father known to men; therefore, since He is about to intercede for those very men to whom He had revealed the Father, He says, "I manifested thy name unto the men whom thou gavest me out of the world."

The particular "name" in question here is "Father." In the

Son, God had revealed Himself as Father, had called upon men to address Him as Father in prayer, and thus had brought to an end the fear toward God that had possessed men's minds under the old covenant; a fear that prevented men from pronouncing the sacred name of God in private prayer, in public worship, and in the reading of Scripture. And to whom had Jesus Christ revealed the Father? To those who had been able to apprehend that revelation: "Unto the men whom thou gavest me out of the world." In the fourth Gospel it is sometimes the Father who gives men to the Son (6:37, 44, 65; 10:29; 17:24; 18:9); at other times it is said to be the Son who chooses them (6:70, 15:16). Both facts are true, but neither the Father nor the Son ever compels men (1:11f., 3:18f., 12:47f.).

And who were those men to whom the Son had manifested the Father's name, and for whom He is about to intercede? (i) They belonged to the Father, therefore it was the Father who gave them to the Son (v. 6); and the Apostles had been given to the Son by the Father in answer to prayer (Luke 6:12f., and see pp. 23f.), and by leading them to Christ (John 6:37, 44). (ii) They had proved unswerving in their loyalty, and faithful to their high calling: "They have kept thy word" (v. 6). This "word" which the Apostles had "kept" was Christ's revelation of the Father, hence the Son here describes it as "thy word" (cf. John 7:16, 12:49). And to keep this word means to store it up in the memory, to obey and fulfill it, to keep it in the heart in order to impart it to others that they might come to know God who has revealed Himself as Father through the Son. (iii) They had persistently believed in Christ and had accepted His words as the very words of God. Jesus' words in verse 7, "Whatsoever thou hast given me," refer to His teaching and mission, as verse 8 confirms; and this the Eleven had received and believed. This was the outcome of their having "kept thy word" (v. 6). They are now convinced that whatsoever the Son had, He had from the Father. They believed Him to be the revelation of the Father, and had clung tenaciously to the conviction that He had been sent from God (vv. 7-8); and this in spite of doubt and discouragement (John 6:67-71, Matt. 16:15-20).

And it was, and still is, only such men who can receive the revelation of the Father, the Father who, through the Incarnate Son, had disclosed Himself to men as love, holiness and righteousness, the Fountainhead of grace and truth. And as Christ had not been able to make God known as a holy and loving Father to everyone He met on earth but only to those whom the Father had given Him, so today not all who hear the Good News respond. Not that the Eleven had fully understood all the words that Jesus had spoken to them. Dull hearts and dark minds made that impossible; but what they had taken serious hold of, in spite of blindness, was this: Jesus of Nazareth had come forth from the Father (John 6:69, 16:30). In other words, so far as they were concerned, Jesus Christ was God manifest in the flesh; and it was upon this impregnable rock of the deity of Christ that they were to build in the future. They had come to this conviction because Jesus had given them the Father's words (v. 8). At a moment in the gospel story there had begun to take firm root in their minds the conviction that Jesus' mission was from the Father. The recurrence, then, of the fivefold solemn reaffirmation in this prayer that the Father had sent Christ (vv. 8, 18, 21, 23, 25), now assumes greater significance. When Jesus could say that they "knew of a truth that I came forth from thee," they no longer doubted the divinity of His mission or the reality of His Messiahship. His words and deeds had proved the first; the second was still a matter of faith, but the resurrection and the ascension clinched the matter.

The words "For the words which thou gavest me I have given unto them" (v. 8) are of great importance for us today. Those who proclaim the gospel throughout the world should ever remember that the words preached were received by Christ from the Father; that He then gave them to the Apostles, who in turn gave them to others; and now these very same words are being heralded forth still. The conviction that these words originated in the mind and heart of the Father should impart an authority that is divine to all proclamation of the gospel.

Small wonder, then, that the next words in Jesus' prayer should express profound concern for the Eleven: "I pray for them: I pray not for the world" (v. 9). The word rendered "pray" here should be noticed. It is *erōtaō*, which, in the fourth Gospel is used only with reference to Christ's prayers to the Father (cf. 14:16; 17:9, 15, 20). The other word used for prayer in John's gospel is *aiteō*, but it is confined to prayers addressed to God by men (e.g., 14:13, 14). In his *New Testament Synonyms*, Trench says that *aiteō* emphasizes the sense of inferiority in the petitioner (as e.g., in Acts 12:20, 3:2); whereas *erōtaō* emphasizes the equality of the person making the request with the one from whom the request is being made. The first conveys the idea of petition, the second of request. The distinction is recognized and maintained throughout the New Testament. When Jesus prays the Father on behalf of the disciples He never petitions, He makes request, as One fully conscious of His equality with the Father. When Martha uses *aiteō* with reference to the prayers of Jesus, that simply demonstrates her lack of understanding of the Person of Christ. Never is *erōtaō* used in the New Testament of a man's prayers to God, with the possible exception of I John 5:16. Notice how the Lord uses both words in John 16:26, but the distinction is carefully maintained: "In that day ye shall ask [*aiteō*] . . . I will pray [*erotaō*] . . . ."

The words "I pray not for the world" mean "I am not now praying for the world." They do not imply that the world is past praying for because an eternal decree of exclusion against sinners has gone forth. This is clear from God's love for the world (John 3:16), from the nature and intention of Jesus' mission (John 4:42, Rom. 5:8), His prayers for sinners on the cross (Luke 23:34), His prayer for the world later in His High-Priestly Prayer (vv. 21, 23), His enjoining the disciples to do likewise (Matt. 5:44, etc.), and His High-Priestly intercession now in glory for sinning men and women (I John 2:1, Rom. 8:34, Heb. 7:25). But the distinction between the Church and the world, and Christ's attitude to each in His prayer are nevertheless significant. When He does pray for the world in verses 21, 23, He prays that it may come to believe in Him and be assured that it was the Father who had sent Him. He could only pray for the world's conversion because it is hostile to the Father (John 8:43, James 4:4). The Apostles, on the other hand, had already come to believe in Jesus and His mission; therefore, not only are His prayers entirely different for them, but at this juncture in His prayer He prays for them and not for the world. They are to be the instruments for evangelizing the world; by their lips and their lives they are to proclaim the Word; He intercedes for them, therefore, that their testimony may prevail, and that while bearing their testimony all their needs may be met.

It was natural that Christ should claim the Father's exclusive regard for the Eleven. Upon this handful of men the future of the Church reposed. They represented the main results of the Lord's earthly ministry. The winning of the world for Him depended upon them. It was not that the Lord was indifferent to the world when He was at prayer in John 17. He longed to save it, but it lay in the power of the evil one (I John 5:19); therefore it had to be penetrated by the gospel. But this could be done only through the witness of the Eleven; therefore, it is for them that He must pray just now, not for the world.

Before doing so the Lord gives three reasons why He should pray exclusively for the apostles. (i) "They are thine" (vv. 9-10); and because they were the Father's it was the Father's responsibility to keep them. They had belonged to the Father originally; now they were the Son's; but that fact only made them the Father's more securely. (ii) "I am glorified in them" (v. 10) by means of their perseverance in faith when others fell away (6:68f.). The words imply that Christ's honor, the success of His cause, the purity and preaching of His gospel, were in their hands: how necessary, then, that the Father should keep them. (iii) "I am no more in the world" (v. 11), and they, therefore, would be left alone in the world; alone in a world that would scorn and hate them because they were Jesus' representatives. In an altogether special sense, then, He must commit them to the Father's safekeeping. In doing so the Lord emphasizes His perfect union with the Father by use of the words "mine . . . thine, thine . . . mine" (v. 10). The "things" which are said to belong equally to the Father and the Son probably refer to the men for whom the Son now prays, as the conclusion of verse 9 suggests. It is not, however, impossible that "things" refer to the divine attributes which, because they belong to the Father, belong also to the Son.

And now, having laid down these three reasons why He should pray for the Eleven in particular, the Lord goes on to present three requests on their behalf.

(i) "Holy Father, keep them in thy name" (v. 11). A name in Scripture often tells not only who its bearer is, but what he is. The name Jesus Christ explains not only what He is in terms of His divine nature and attributes, but also who He is in terms of His relations with us. But now it is the name Father that is referred to, the name which God gave to the Son to reveal to the disciples; and to that revealed name the Son prays that the Apostles should be kept true. They are to be preserved in the knowledge of God's name as Father. As His sons they call Him Father; in virtue of that relation they are His possession, and therefore nothing can harm them. As they live under this divine protection in an antagonistic world they bear the Father's name as His witnesses.

The title "Holy Father" occurs only here in Scripture. Its

use is appropriate at this point because the Son is asking the Holy Father to keep the disciples in an unholy world (cf. v. 15); and they would be kept through the Son's holiness, which the Father will be asked to give them (v. 17), holiness being the divine attribute above all others by which the apostles would be protected from the corrupting influences of an unholy world. In a sense this petition is the most fundamental in Christ's prayer. Since the Eleven retained the knowledge of God which Jesus had given them, they would be one as the Father and the Son are one. It is as Father that God in Christ draws men to Himself, but it is as *Holy* Father that He does this; therefore those who are drawn must also be holy. Holy love is the supreme trait in the divine character, so Christ asks the Father to keep vigil over the Eleven and hold them secure in the embrace of that holy love. The world would be a dangerous place for them without the companionship of Jesus Christ, but with the protection of the Father's name about them they would prove that "the name of Jehovah is a strong tower; the righteous runneth into it and is safe" (Prov. 18:10).

(ii) The second petition is in verse 11: "That they may be one." Here a new bond of union among the disciples is referred to. There was already in existence an organic unity based upon oneness of belief, but what was lacking was oneness of spirit, of will and of purpose (Luke 22:24, John 13:4-15), through union with Christ in the Holy Spirit. This spiritual union was about to be effected. Once it was established, and consequently the oneness which it in turn would introduce among the disciples, it would be seen to conform to the essential perfect spiritual union between the Father and the Son. Underlying the oneness of will and love that would one day bind the apostles into one, there would be the unity effected by the indwelling of the Spirit of Christ (I Cor. 6:17), a unity or oneness of nature (II Pet. 1:4); a unity without which their witness would fail (John 15:8, 12), because there is little difference between a divided church and a divided world. The great danger confronting the Eleven would be the disruption of the fellowship that bound each to each, and all to Christ. Indeed, soon after Pentecost the disruptive forces of doctrinal differences (Acts 15:1-29), and of the clash of personalities (Acts 15:36-41), began to manifest themselves in the infant Church. How appropriate, then, is Christ's prayer that the Father should keep them that they may be one. And the Father is to keep them in truth and in love; in truth because that was what they were to proclaim to the world, and in love because it was love that was to govern all their relationships with each other. As they were kept by the Father in truth, doctrine would be kept pure; and as they were kept in truth, the Eleven who held the truth would love each other and those to whom the saving truth was to be proclaimed.

The Lord continues to think about the keeping of the disciples by declaring that He has been doing in the past three years what He now asks the Father to do. "I kept them in thy name" (v. 12). The word "kept" should be rendered "was keeping," the tense in Greek signifying Christ's continual watching over the disciples. Judas was, of course, the single exception, but the disposition of this man had singled him out from the beginning for his tragic end. Not even the keeping power of the Son of God could save a man whom Jesus Himself could describe as "the son of perdition" (v. 12). The phrase means "he who is destined to perdition." It occurs once more in the New Testament (II Thess. 2:3), with reference to "the man of sin." Not that the Lord had abandoned Judas soon after he joined the disciple band. Indeed, for three years He had labored and prayed to save him from spiritual suicide. Right up to the last, even in the upper room, He sought to "keep" Judas. But all to no avail. Christ did not lose Judas (cf. 18:9); Judas lost himself. How different was Peter's case! Peter was even to deny his Lord, but there was an inherent quality in his character that made possible his rescue from the abyss.

And in being kept the Eleven were to share Jesus Christ's own indestructible joy in the midst of sorrow (v. 13). "My joy" means "the joy that is mine" (3:29, 15:11). The construction is also used of Christ's peace (14:27, 16:33), Christ's judgment (14:15), Christ's love (15:10), and Christ's glory (17:24). The joy in verse 13 was that which Jesus experienced in fellowship with the Father (15:11, I John 1:4). It was also the joy that He derived from performing completely the Father's will; the joy that His mission was about to issue in triumph (15:11), and that He was about to bring the Church into being; the joy that was now sustaining Him as He moved forward to the Cross. Now He prays that the Eleven might be sustained and comforted by this same joy.

And this is the joy that He communicates to the Church still. The following verses in John 17 describe how the joy that is Christ's "is fulfilled" in the Church's experience. She finds this joy in answering the Savior's call to proclaim to the world the word of life, she finds joy through the Spirit of holiness which differentiates her from the world and yet which involves her in responsibility to the world, she finds joy in being kept from the world's standards of judgment and modes of conduct, and thus acts as the salt of the earth. As the Church realizes that the Lord is with her in the Holy Spirit to protect her, she rejoices "in hope of the glory of God" (Rom. 5:2).

Christ has still one more request to make of the Father on behalf of the Eleven, but before presenting it He lays down two further reasons why the Father should keep them — so important was the keeping of the disciples by the Father in His mind. (a) "I have given them thy word" (v. 14). As in earlier verses, "thy word" means the total revelation of the Father, and this self-disclosure of God as Father in the Son, Jesus had communicated to them. How supremely important, therefore, that the Father should protect them. (b) "The world hated them" (v. 14); therefore they would need to be kept by the Father. But why should the world hate those men so? Because "thy word," the revelation of God as Father (v. 14), had entered their hearts, and had made them the kind of men for whom the world has neither time nor patience. The entrance of this divine word had created within their minds spiritual values that condemned the values that operated in the world; therefore it hated the disciples as it had hated their Lord. It was because of this word that they were not of the world; neither in origin nor in character.

And now in verse 15 Christ explains what He meant when, in verse 11, He asked the Father to keep the disciples. The Father was to keep them safe, not by taking them out of the world, but by keeping them from contamination while they continued in the world. The Father's protection does not mean that they were to be kept immune from enemy attack in the form of persecution or temptation, but that they were to be preserved from constant pressure from the enemy. Only thus could they do God's work, and be sanctified by God's truth. They were to be kept, not from moral conflict, but from moral evil.

But what made the Father's protection necessary at all? While the evil one had found nothing in Christ (John 14:30), he had, alas, found something in the Eleven. There was something in their nature that enabled him to gain a foothold and work his evil designs and create havoc in their lives. Proof of this is in Luke 9:54, 22:24, and in Peter's denial. When the Son, therefore, asks the Father to keep the disciples He means, not only protection from contact with evil, but also liberation from the evil one, since evil is conceived to be personal (cf. I John 2:13; 3:10, 12; 5:18f.; and cf. John 3:12, II Thess. 3:13). The relation between the Christian and good and evil is personal, not impersonal; but he is "in Christ," and while he lives and moves and has his being in Christ he is, of necessity, kept "out of" (which is the force of "from" in v. 15) the evil one. Contact without contamination is what Christ asks for in this prayer. For the Christian to be *of* the world is unthinkable, but he must be *in* the world, to give his witness *to* the world. He is kept from *conformity to* the world, but not from *concern for* the world. The truth, as it was honored and obeyed, would keep the Eleven from conformity to the world, but the same truth had to be proclaimed to the world, even though the world would hate them for it. "In the world, but not of the world": there we have what Archbishop Temple called the "dilemma of demarcation" between the Christian and the world. The hermit is wrong, but so also is the worldly Christian: but where to draw the line of true adjustment between the two! That is the crux of a problem that every Christian must solve for himself before God. All that Jesus does in this verse is to lay down the double principle — "in the world, but not of the world" — and He leaves us to work it out under the guidance of the Holy Spirit.

(iii) And now comes the third request that Christ made on behalf of the Eleven. It is in verse 17. The world's hatred of the Christian (v. 14) is, in verse 16, the basis of the Lord's request that the Father should protect the disciples; in verse 17 it is the basis of His request that the Father should sanctify them. The world's hatred of the believer necessitates not his removal from the world, but his preservation from pollution and his sanctification. The word sanctification has, of course, reference to personal holiness. To sanctify means to consecrate, set apart persons or things to God (Ex. 28:41; 29:1, 36; 40:13; cf. also I Thess. 5:23). This work of sanctification is effected through the truth, the truth being both the sphere within which the work takes place, and the instrument with which the work is effected. In addition, there is the activity of the purifying Spirit within the Christian, and the external conflicts and afflictions to which the Christian is subjected. But in Jesus' request in verse 17 the principal agent in the Christian's sanctification is the truth, God's word, in its subjective inner power.

But in addition to this aspect, sanctification may also have reference to spiritual endowment and equipment for service, as indeed the context here suggests. It is conjoined with the witness that the disciples were to give to the world. The word is also used in John 10:36, of the Son's being set apart by the Father, and it is the setting apart for mission that is prominent, as in 17:17. The mission of the Eleven was to represent Christ, and the instrument by which they would fulfill this mission was to be the truth, the Father's word, the revelation of God as Father. The truth was to be the realm in which they were to live, and the instrument by which they were to work. Archbishop Temple, in his Commentary on St. John's Gospel, points out that "sanctify in Greek describes the dedication of a sacrificial victim, or the setting apart of a person for religious service"; and this is probably the idea that the word conveys in John 17:17. To state the matter otherwise: it is not the nature of the thing dedicated that is in view here, but rather the *act* of dedicating it for sacred use; although, naturally, that very act of dedication implies both fitness of character and ability for the sacred duty to which the person is dedicated.

This was probably in the Lord's mind when He prayed, "Sanctify them in the truth." So far as character was concerned, the disciples had been fitted for the service for which they were to be commissioned. This work in their characters had been effected through the purifying power of the word (15:3). Now that this work has been accomplished the Son requests the Father to sanctify (i.e., consecrate) them to the work they are about to undertake. In this sense the word "sanctify" has reference both to the Father's purpose for the Apostles and to the equipment necessary to enable them to fulfill that purpose.

That "sanctify" means "consecrate to or for service" is clear from verse 18, the subject of which is the mission which the Son came to perform, and which the Eleven are now to continue: "As thou didst send me into the world, even so sent I them into the world." Obviously the sense of mission is very pronounced. And because the Son was sending the disciples forth, they would require the same equipment as He had received — divine illumination, wisdom, courage and, above all, the presence and power of the Holy Spirit. They would require identical equipment because their mission was identical. It was a continuation of the one abiding mission of the Father. The same word for "send" occurs in connection with the Apostles' original mission (Mark 3:14), their special mission (Luke 9:2), and the renewal of their original mission in John 20:21f., where John 17:18 received its fulfillment. Christ did not leave the Eleven in the world, He *sent* them to the world.

"Sanctify" in the sense of equipment for service occurs again in verse 19, where the Father's sending the Son into the world on His mission is linked with the Son's sanctifying Himself, or consecrating Himself. And, of course, the sinless Son of God's personal sanctification would have reference, not to personal fitness or holiness, but to His willing and implicit obedience to the Father for the fulfillment of the Father's mission. We are probably justified, then, in understanding the Lord's use of the word "sanctify" in this prayer, both of Himself and the Eleven, in the sense of equipment for service. This makes verse 17 more meaningful, and verse 19 easier to understand. The latter verse would mean that Jesus' consecrating Himself to His mission in the world makes possible the disciples' consecrating themselves to their mission. His consecrating Himself to die for the sins of the whole world, and to make possible the consecration of the Christian, means that both His sacrifice and His consecration to that sacrifice were mediatorial in that they mediated salvation and the consecration of those who believe.

It is necessary, however, to underline the difference between Christ's consecration and the Christian's. The Son consecrates Himself, but He must ask the Father to consecrate the disciples. True, in John 10:36 the Father consecrates the Son, but there the similarity ends. The Christian's sanctification, or consecration, necessitates what Christ's never did — redemption and purification from sin. The Son consecrated Himself when the Father sanctified Him to the Father's mission. Now while the Son's personal consecration of Himself makes the Christian's consecration possible, it can never take the place of the Christian's personal dedication to God. The first makes the second possible; it should also make it inevitable, since Christ's blood saves the sinner and consecrates him to the mission the Father allots to him. While, therefore, we cannot consecrate ourselves, we may dedicate ourselves to God that He might consecrate us: hence Jesus' petition, "Sanctify them." Only Jesus Christ can say, "I sanctify myself" (v. 19).

> Consecrate me now to Thy service, Lord,
> By the power of grace divine.

3. Jesus Christ in prayer before the Father on behalf of the whole Church (vv. 20-24). The main thoughts in this section of the prayer are: the necessity for the conversion of those who

are still "of the world"; their consequent union with the Father through the Son and the indwelling Spirit; their communion with each other on the basis of this union with the Father, the Son, and the Holy Spirit, manifested in forms sufficiently concrete to convince the world that Christ is the Savior; and the ultimate vision of the glory of the Son in which the Church will participate at the end of the age.

In this part of the prayer the Lord intercedes "for them also that believe on me through their [the disciples'] word" (v. 20). This is a natural step after His request for the disciples' consecration, and their being sent forth on the Father's mission. The Eleven were only the first fruit, the "earnest" of the Church that was yet to be. "Through their word," that is to say, through their preaching and witnessing, others were to come to faith in Christ. Since, then, the Lord has in view the whole Church throughout history we are justified in finding a place for ourselves and for those who will come after us, in this prayer.

Only one petition is made for the Church throughout the ages: "That they may all be one" (vv. 21, 22). This is the design or intention of the Son's prayer for the Church; and the urgency with which we should consider this prayer of Jesus lies in this, that it is through the witness of a united Church that men believe in Christ, and are in turn added to the Church. And how are believers to be "one"? Not through conference and committee, not through discussion and exchange of views, though these undoubtedly have their place. These are the effect, not the cause of union. The cause of oneness is personal union with the Father, through the Son, and through the work of the Spirit in the heart thus united with the Father. This is clear from an early reading of verse 21: "That they may all be one . . . that they also may be *in* us" (cf. 6:56, 15:4f.). That is the basis of the spiritual union for which Christ prays here. Those who are in the Father and in the Son through the indwelling Spirit are all one in Christ Jesus.

Now the norm of this spiritual unity between Christians is the unity between the Father and the Son: "Even as thou, Father, art in me, and I in thee" (v. 21). Not only is the unity in the Godhead the norm, it is also the ground of the Church's oneness: "That they also may be [one] in us" (v. 21). The same truth is expressed in verse 23: "I in them, and thou in me, that they may be perfected into one."

Obviously, then, the union to which Christ refers here transcends mere external unity. Its center of gravity is not earth but heaven. The world is not convinced that Christ came from the Father when the Church issues a statement of unity in doctrine, practice, and purpose. And because this is a spiritual union that finds its counterpart in the union of the Father and the Son, no outward disunity can break it. The presence of the Holy Spirit in every Christian's heart, and the oneness of purpose and doctrine, unite the Church indissolubly, denominations notwithstanding. Where one, or all, of the marks of spiritual oneness is lacking, no external union, no matter how impressive, will convince the world. It is unity in one Master, one message, one mission, that convinces the world that the Father sent Jesus Christ into the world. Sectarianism is condemned by Jesus' request in verse 21; differences in forms of Church government and worship are not. These may be compatible with unity in the apostolic message and mission. Outward union, or formal attachment, cannot produce spiritual union because spiritual union is "in," not "with" Christ; its unifying principle, as well as its ideal, is in the unity of the Father and the Son. This oneness, however, must manifest itself visibly, and therefore every Christian is obligated to pray and work for a greater visible manifestation of this invisible union, that the world may recognize the Church's spiritual oneness, and may come to believe that Jesus Christ is the Son whom the Father sent into the world.

Having made the request for the oneness of the Eleven, and then for the whole Church, Christ now gives three reasons for the request, reasons which transcend any consideration such as the unity being highly desirable in itself. (i) "That the world may believe that thou didst send me" (v. 21). The oneness of the elect is not an end in itself. The Father sent the Son, the Son sent the Eleven, the Eleven sent their converts, and we are now being sent — all for one identical purpose; that the world might know, and then believe, that the Father sent the Son. This is both the world's need and the world's hope, but a disunited Church cannot give an effective witness to a disrupted world, because it is

> ... with a *scornful* wonder,
> Men see her sore oppressed;
> By schisms rent asunder;
> By heresies distressed.

(ii) The second reason for this request of Jesus is: "The glory which thou hast given me I have given unto them; that they may be one" (v. 2). Having prayed for the Church's oneness, Christ now refers to what He has done to make this union possible: He has given the Church the glory which the Father gave Him. The Father gave the Son this glory in connection with the accomplishment of the world's redemption, the glory that was manifested in the Son's resurrection and ascension, and in His reception of all authority (v. 24). This glory Christ now gives to the Church. As communicated to the Church this glory is, in the words of H. B. Swete, "the glory of the divine character," of which love is the essential feature; or as Archbishop Temple puts it, "glory" here is "absolute love in perfect self-surrender." But however one may attempt to define this glory that Jesus Christ gives to the Church, it is manifested in the Church's union within herself, and in her love for the world; naturally, then, the manifestation of Christ's glory within the Church contributes in turn to Christ's glory in the world when, through the Church's unity and love, men believe in Him. Here, then, is an added condemnation of a divided Church — she cannot contribute as she ought to the glory of her Lord.

But to what purpose is the communication of this glory if the Church is disunited? The answer is the third reason why Christ requests the Father to make the Church's oneness effective: "That the world may know that thou didst send me, and lovedst them, even as thou lovedst me" (v. 23). Christ communicates His glory to the Church that she may be perfected into one, and the world come to believe that God sent Jesus Christ. The Greek tense implies that the world may keep on knowing that the Father loves the world. Proof of the Father's love for the world is His having sent the Son into the world; and this love of the Father becomes in turn an illustration of how Christians ought to love each other and the world to whom Christ has sent her. Here, then, is yet another condemnation of a disrupted Church — disunity slows down the work of evangelizing the world, because it is through her oneness that the Church convinces the world that Jesus Christ, and the Christian faith, are divine. The Church cannot escape the dilemma of her disunity by pleading that her oneness is essentially spiritual and invisible. That is undoubtedly true, since it is of the same essence as the oneness in the Godhead: but that invisible union must manifest itself in concrete fashion, and it may well be that our Lord's prayer for the Church's oneness included, or evisaged, this concrete and visible embodiment of the spiritual union of the Body of Christ. It is when the world *sees* the spiritual union of the Church in concrete form that it believes that Jesus Christ was the Son sent by the Father.

4. The Lord, who has been interceding with the Father on behalf of the Eleven, the whole Church, and the world, now brings His prayer to a close. This final division (vv. 24-26) is an epilogue thrown into the form of a petition which the Son addresses to the Father. It is in two parts: (i) Christ prays that the whole Church be reunited in glory with her Lord; (ii) He prays for the Church militant who, because of her union with the Lord, is separated from the world. In addition, the epilogue underlines the uniqueness of Christ the Son of God, who reveals the Father's nature, who is the supreme object of the Father's love, and in whom the Church will be gathered into the perfect eternal oneness in glory.

(i) For a brief moment, the Lord lifts His eyes to pierce through the gloom of the present hour to future glory. His use of the name "Father" brings into prominence the relation between Him the eternal Son, and the Father blessed for ever. It is upon this blessed relation that Jesus Christ places His final request in this prayer. Because God is His Father in an absolute sense (11:41, 12:27, Matt. 11:27), He can say in His prayer, "I will" (v. 24). On several occasions Jesus exercised His will (21:22, Matt. 8:3, 23:27, 26:29, Luke 12:49), but there was always perfect harmony between His will and the Father's. What Christ wills in prayer here has already been granted in anticipation (v. 22); now He wills that it become a reality. Jesus' will was always perfectly identified with the will of the Father, even when His human will seemed to conflict with the Father's, as in Gethsemane (Mark 14:36, and see pp. 42ff.).

And what is it that the Son wills in His prayer? "That they also whom thou hast given me be with me where I am, that they may behold my glory" (v. 24). This is the grand purpose lying behind the creating of the Body of Christ. Indeed, the whole Church united together, which is the Father's gift to the Son, may be said to constitute this glory that the Father bestowed upon the Son. This is, so to speak, the completion of the glory the Father gave the Son in resurrection and ascension; that is why the Son prays, "That they may behold my glory." And yet not, "my glory," but rather, "my glory which thou hast given me" (v. 24). It is true that St. John, speaking of Christ, says, "We beheld his glory" (1:14); but even that was "the glory of the only begotten of the Father." And speaking in anticipation here in verse 24 the Lord remarks that this glory has already been given to Him; and by an exercise of His will He desires that believers should share it with Him. The Father has given the Son both the glory (v. 24) and the men for whom He has been praying (v. 11); and now He wills that the first should be shared by the second.

The word "behold" in verse 24 implies not apprehension by faith, but the actual beholding by the Church of the glory of her triumphant Lord. What it will mean actually to share Christ's glory is summed up in II Timothy 2:12: "We shall also reign with him." And the effect of this beholding of Christ's glory is described in I John 3:2: "We shall see him even as he is," when "we shall be like him." The words "where I am" (v. 24) mean to be with Christ in glory; to see Jesus honored and supreme is joy enough for the Christian, but to have a share in His glory will be joy unspeakable. The Church, blemished by imperfections and divisions today, will tomorrow be presented by Jesus Christ to the Father, without spot or wrinkle; and she, beholding the ineffable glory of her Lord, will be transformed into the same image, from glory to glory.

(ii) In the second part of this concluding section of the prayer Christ turns his eyes back again from that still unfulfilled vision of future glory to the stark realities of the present. He looks at the Eleven upon whom so much depends. He takes a last look around the room that has been re-echoing to His voice and within whose shadows eleven mystified men have been crouching. He must go now. The crushing sorrow of Gethsemane awaits Him, and implacable enemies, and a rough wooden cross, and the nameless horror for which it stood; but as He goes forth to face all that, it is in the certainty that He has already overcome the world (16:33).

And so He brings His prayer to a close. As we close our prayers by saying, "For Jesus Christ's sake," or, "Through Jesus Christ our Lord," or, "In the name of Jesus Christ our Lord," so in presenting His prayer to the Father the Son pleads two things: (a) The righteousness of the eternal Father: "O righteous Father," He cries (v. 25). Here the Son appeals to the absolute justice and truth of the Father, hence the title "Righteous Father." He appeals to the justice of the Father when asking that Christians may not share the fate of the impenitent, just as in an earlier section of this prayer He appealed to the holiness of the Father by using the title "Holy Father" (v. 11). (b) The Son, however, also pleads His own faithfulness in accomplishing the mission the Father had given Him to fulfill: "I made known unto them thy name" (v. 26). We understand that in addition to the Father's righteousness, the Son pleads His own merits.

And what was this work that Jesus Christ has now accomplished? He says, "I knew thee" (v. 25), through direct vision, of course; but He is able to add, "I made known thy name unto them" (v. 26). Notice the simple statements of fact in verse 25f.; the world knew not God, Jesus Christ knew Him, the Apostles knew that God had sent Him, Christ has made God's name known to them. But while the Lord has made this revelation to the disciples, in another sense the revelation is inexhaustible, both in content and meaning; therefore, He adds "and will make it known." How? Through the Holy Spirit, who will continue to instruct succeeding generations of Christians (14:26, 16:13). The declaring of the Ineffable Name to each generation is the great mission in which Jesus Christ, through the Holy Spirit, is perpetually engaged (16: 12, 25); a mission that is identical with that in which He was engaged in His incarnate life (17:6).

As for the Eleven, the love with which the Father had loved the Son was to be in them; and the Son Himself, through the Holy Spirit, would dwell in them (v. 26). The purpose lying behind the revealing of the Ineffable Name to each Christian is that the Father's love may dwell in the heart. There is a great interdependence between knowledge of the Father and love for the Father in that the knowledge depends upon the degree in which the love operates in the heart (I John 4:8).

The three last words in the prayer, "I in them," are at once the crown and the summary of the entire prayer. The indwelling presence of Christ in the heart is the golden thread that links the upper-room discourses together; it is now the link that connects these discourses to the High-Priestly Prayer, and makes of both a glorious unity. The main conviction that would take hold of the minds of the Eleven after they had heard the discourses and the prayer would be that they and Christ could never be separated. Physically absent, yes; spiritually absent, never. His presence was unseen but it was real. Up till this moment they had known Christ after the flesh and were, therefore, outside Him; now they were to know Him after the flesh no more. They were to know Him after the Spirit, and were to have Him dwelling in their hearts for ever. The indwelling of Jesus Christ in the hearts of the Eleven was to be the most outstanding evidence of His love for them (v. 26).

With that great assurance Jesus Christ can now rest afresh in the love and faithfulness of the Father, and bring His prayer to a close. His work for the Eleven is completed so far as His earthly life is concerned; and He has asked for His own dear ones all that they will need in respect of essential spiritual blessing. But He must now go forth to complete the Father's mission on behalf of the whole world. And so He slips out into the night with His "little flock of loyal hearts"; out to tread the road to Gethsemane and Calvary. That was a dark road, but it led to ultimate victory. At its end He stood the Savior of the world, and the Eternal Christ of all our Easter mornings.

This, then, is an example of Christ's prayers, and its main features should be a guide for all who are pupils in His school of prayer. It is direct in its method, and simple in its language; it is orderly in its design, and practical in its intention; it is brief in its compass, and intimate in its approach; it is unselfish in its requests, and profound in its principles. Its general theme is the oneness of the Church, and the glory of Christ, in which the Church will one day share. It constitutes the consecration of the Son to the Father's mission. It unveils the sources of Christ's joy — the absolute supremacy of the Father's will, obedience to the Father's will, the unswerving loyalty of the Eleven, the faith of future believers, the ultimate triumph of the Church. Its over-riding concerns are the Father's protection and assistance for the disciples, the renewal of the Son's consecration to the Father for the work still to be accomplished, the Son's gratitude to the Father for enabling Him to glorify the Father, the revelation of God as Father through the Son, the oneness of the Father with the Son and the Father's love for the Son, and the manifestation of that oneness and love in the Church's life and witness, and the coming of the world to a knowledge of the deity of Christ and the divinity of the Church's faith through that oneness and love in the Church.

Here in very truth the Lord Jesus Christ draws aside the veil to show us the nature of His communion with the Father. This prayer may be taken as part of His answer to our petition, "Lord, teach us to pray." When the great principles that came to expression in our Lord's prayers begin to operate in ours, then we shall begin to understand what prayer really is.

CHAPTER FOUR

THE LORD'S PRAYER

THE USUAL DESIGNATION given to the prayer in Matthew 6:9-13 is "The Lord's Prayer," but this title does not, of course, occur in the New Testament. Its use here is not to be taken to imply that the prayer so described was one that Christ Himself used. The request for forgiveness in verse 12 rules out completely that possibility. The designation as used here implies simply that the words of this prayer came originally from the mind and heart of our Lord.

In the verses preceding the prayer in Matthew 6, Christ had just been giving directions concerning prayer. These directions represented a totally new point of departure in prayer, and a completely fresh view of prayer. In His teaching Jesus had emphasized the necessity for sincerity, secrecy, simplicity and serenity in prayer (Matt. 6:5-8). Now He goes on to give His disciples an example of what He conceived real prayer to be. This prayer was not simply an illustration of Christian prayer; it was given as a set form of prayer which should be used. Matthew reports our Lord as saying, "After *this manner* therefore pray ye" (6:9); while Luke is even more definite in 11:2, where the Lord says, "When ye pray, *say*." Obviously, however, this form of prayer is not to become a fetish; otherwise, after having in His teaching on prayer broken the chains that had reduced prayer to a slavish, mechanical system, Christ would have forged a still heavier fetter.

From the point of view both of form and content, then, this is a prayer that must be used by Christians until the end of the age. It gathers up in concise fashion the various things for which believers should pray. It is, at the same time, a pattern of the spirit, the aims, and the proportions of true prayer. It is a prayer that gives prominence to God. Only after God's glory has been given proper place does it concern itself with the needs of men. It begins with worship, which is the highest activity of which the spirit of man is capable; and the One who is worshipped is a heavenly Father who is omnipotent. Those, therefore, who worship Him will necessarily be reverent before Him; they will be concerned to become the instruments through whom God's kingdom will come; and they will earnestly desire to be obedient to God's will. These will be their first considerations in prayer, not their claims upon their heavenly Father's benevolence, nor their need for His sustenance, His forbearance and forgiveness, His protection in present and future circumstances. We must put first things first in prayer, and not invert the spiritual order which is so clearly expressed in this prayer.

The Lord's Prayer occurs twice in the gospel records: in Matthew 6:9-13, and in Luke 11:2-4. In each the context is different. In Matthew it is preceded by a passage in which our Lord teaches men what true and efficacious prayer is; in Luke the prayer is Christ's response to a request from one of the disciples for guidance on how to pray, a request that was prompted by the sight of the Son of God Himself at prayer. And, as has already been suggested, this prayer which the Lord gave His disciples has a quite definite form. It is neither shapeless nor haphazard. Not only so, but the form is exceedingly simple. It consists of three parts. First there is a short invocation (Matt. 6:9a, Luke 11:2a). This is followed by six petitions which, again be it noted, follow an orderly and natural sequence (Matt. 6:9b-13a, Luke 11:2b-4). There Luke's report of the prayer ends, but Matthew's account includes, in the third place, a doxology (6:13b). In other words, we have in Matthew's Gospel a prayer that includes invocation, petition, and doxology. Now, since Matthew's form of the prayer is the more complete, we shall use it for our study here.

First, we must have regard to the context in which the evangelist places it. A cursory glance over the prayer as given by Matthew leaves one with the impression that it does not fit into the context in which it is found in the first Gospel. Matthew, however, does make it an integral part of the Sermon on the Mount, and on closer examination it is seen to be a summary of that Sermon, the quintessence of the profoundest principles contained in the discourse. Here in unforgettable language the meaning of the Fatherhood of God is made clear; as are also the claims of the divine Father upon His children, and theirs upon Him, in virtue of the Father-son relationship that binds them together in the bond of the new covenant established by the blood of Christ. In this prayer there comes to unique expression that spirit of sonship which Jesus Christ has been underlining throughout the Sermon. To offer this prayer, therefore, in sincerity and in truth is to signify that one is a child of God and a disciple of Christ;

and because the prayer is the quintessence of those things that distinguish the Christian from the non-Christian, it is in very truth the prayer of the Christian Church, not that of the world.

The writer of these pages has read somewhere that there are three main divisions in Matthew's context of the Lord's Prayer; and these should engage our attention because they provide us with a convenient framework within which to study the prayer: (a) the verses which precede the Lord's Prayer (5-8) offer guidance on the preparation for prayer; (b) the terms of the Prayer (9-13) are to be taken as the pattern for prayer; (c) the verses which conclude this section of Matthew's Gospel (14-15) are a reflection upon the prayer just given and, therefore, teach the value of pause after prayer.

PREPARATION FOR PRAYER

There were three outstanding features of Jewish piety and devotion, and these are all referred to by our Lord in the context within which the prayer He gave the Apostles is set. The first was almsgiving (6:1-4), the second was prayer (6:6-15), and the third was fasting (6:16-18). The first reminded the pious Jew of his obligation to help the destitute, the second of his own need for communion with God, and the third of the necessity for a broken and a contrite heart. And these traits should be characteristic of Christian piety today. In Matthew 5 Jesus has set forth our life of sonship with God our heavenly Father, and now in chapter 6 He shows how that life of sonship must manifest itself in acts of piety and devotion — almsgiving, prayer, and fasting. But these, in common with all outward religious practices, lend themselves to abuse, the commonest of which is to practice them in order to win the approval of men: hence the need for preparation of heart before engaging in prayer.

Prayer is essentially communion between God and man. When we consider, therefore, who God is (the Perfection of holiness, glory, wisdom, love and power) and who we are (sinful, finite, ignorant, selfish, weak creatures) we shall realize increasingly the need for preparation of heart and mind and spirit before we seek to commune with God. This preparation should include searching of heart by the Holy Spirit under the light that breaks from the Scriptures, confession of the sins and failures which come to light during this period of heart searching, cleansing from those transgressions through the efficacy of the blood of

Christ, and stirring up the heart to resolve not to let God go until He blesses in prayer.

In addition to those general principles that operate during this period of moral, spiritual, and mental preparation that should precede prayer, there are four others to which Jesus refers in this short passage preceding the Lord's Prayer.

(i) Sincerity: "When ye pray, ye shall not be as the hypocrites" (Matt. 6:5). No matter what a man's religious faith is the danger of hypocrisy in prayer is always present. It was certainly an ever present danger in Judaism, as it is in Islam and other religious faiths. The very posture which every devout Jew adopted in prayer could very easily open the door to insincerity. His obligation to stand when praying with his face toward the Temple in Jerusalem, his head covered, and his eyes downcast could easily become an ostentatious pose which enabled the insincere to appear sincere in their prayers. And doubtless it was this danger that led Christ to distinguish so clearly between real and unreal devotion; and it is in order to purge our hearts from all such insincerity in prayer that this preparatory period should be observed.

We must, above all things, in this preparatory period, set our hearts on being ourselves when we pray. Reality, honesty, sincerity, are the hallmark of true prayer. Prayer that is a parade, a stage play, is hypocrisy. We must, therefore, during the preparation that precedes prayer, determine to cleanse our hearts of all pretense, and, supremely, to be ourselves at the throne of grace. It is during this period of heart preparation that we realize afresh what it is that differentiates real devotion from the false: the first has God alone for its motive. "The secret of religion is religion in secret."

(ii) Secrecy: "And having shut thy door, pray" (Matt. 6:6). The shut door is, of course, essential to the sincere heart. Sincerity and secrecy are indissoluble in prayer. Not that this always involves the physical separation of ourselves from our fellows. It is possible to enter into the inner closet of the heart, to shut the door of the secret chamber of the soul, in the midst of a milling multitude, and of jangling machinery and bewildering perplexities; but the habit of physical withdrawal, as well as of mental detachment, is necessary for the attainment of the true secrecy in prayer for which Christ pleads here.

That is not to say that the Lord disparaged public worship. Indeed, He commanded it both by precept and practice. And even in this prayer that He gave to the Twelve social prayer is underlined by the use of the pronouns "we" and "our." Nor is Jesus casting aspersions upon the usual postures adopted by pious Jews at that time. Here again, it is not the pose but the motive that determines the use of the pose in public prayer — to be seen of men is what is being condemned. By its very nature prayer is essentially the individual's communion with God, and to permit prayer to be affected by unworthy motives and insincere attitudes is to pervert prayer.

Prayers offered in the synagogue or on the market place, or at the street corners — the places where men congregate, and where plenty of spectators could be assured — had constantly to be subjected to the searching test of private prayer, namely, the test of sincerity. Public prayer divorced from private prayer tended inevitably to become a system, a system of hours, postures, methods, and mechanics. If prayers offered in the synagogue and on the street were going to be real they had to be the expression of the heart of a man accustomed to praying "in secret." Only the reality of "praying in secret" could safeguard the sincerity of praying in public. The shut door symbolizes the exclusion of distractions, and ensures that liberty, privacy, spontaneity, and spirituality, which are the soul of prayer "in secret." And have we not seen that the Lord was speaking from personal experience when He laid this injunction upon the disciples? He Himself withdrew from men, and lingered behind the shut door within the inner chamber, to pray to the Father "who is in secret."

(iii) Simplicity: "And in praying use not vain repetitions, as the Gentiles do" (Matt. 6:7). Notice it is not the repeating of prayers that Christ is reproving (some communions of the Church have been doing that for centuries), nor is it the repeating of requests and petitions (Jesus repeated the same words in prayer in Gethsemane), nor is it much praying (again, the Lord passed whole nights in prayer); it is "vain repetitions" that are condemned. They were "vain" because couched in empty, idle, meaningless mumble-jumble, which the petitioner might conceive to act as a charm. The view that prayers prevail if they are sufficiently numerous, and offered with suitable earnestness, is pagan.

The heathen used "vain repetitions" because of their conception of the gods to whom they prayed, and because of their view of what prayer was. They assumed that the deities they worshipped possessed the vices and virtues of their worshippers. They were convinced that by endless repetition, and the multiplication of words, they could weary their gods into granting their requests. The gods, so the pagans conceived, were fickle in their friendship, cynical in their concern for men, critical in their appreciation of worship, unpredictable in their reactions, petulant in their emotions, unstable in their "moral" relations, and capricious in their moods. Naturally, then, the worshippers of those whimsical, mercurial, quasi-moral gods, deities at once noble and crafty, benevolent and malicious, in their control of human fortunes, had perforce to use "vain repetitions" in their devotions. They were convinced that "their much speaking" was essential to a favorable response to their prayers.

Christian prayer, on the other hand, must be purged of all such heathen opinions and practices. Unworthy conceptions of prayer are based on unworthy conceptions of God. The Lord does not hear a prayer because it is of requisite length, and has been re-peated the required number of times. He hears prayer when it is a genuine expression of faith. It is, as we shall see presently, to a loving, holy, unchanging, omnipotent, omniscient heavenly Father that we pray: we must not, therefore, pray "as the Gentiles do," using "vain repetitions" because convinced that God needs to be instructed in our needs.

(iv) Serenity: "Your Father knoweth what things ye have need of, before ye ask him" (Matt. 6:8). As has just been remarked we do not pray in order to supply God with information about our wants or our needs; we pray because it enables us to enter into communion with our heavenly Father who knows our needs (Matt. 6:8), our frame (Ps. 103:14), our hearts (I John 3:20f.), and our burdens (Ps. 55:22, I Pet. 5:7). And it is "your Father" who knoweth these things. When predicated of God the words, "He knows" might engender fear in the mind of the sinner; but when that unqualified statement "He knows" is modified by additional words, and reads:

> He knows, He loves, He cares;
> Nothing this truth can dim;
> He gives the very best to those
> Who leave the choice with Him . . .

then the heart that is lifted up in prayer is careful about nothing, prayerful about everything, thankful for everything; and over that heart the peace of God stands guard (Phil. 4:6f.).

To such a heart the "vain repetitions" referred to in verse 7 are seen to be not only unnecessary but absurd. But if our heav-enly "Father knoweth what things [we] have need of, before [we] ask him," does that not render prayer unnecessary? No, because the Lord has so ordered things that, in principle, He gives to those who ask. Hence, if we desire "good things," we shall ask them from Him from whom cometh down every good and every perfect gift. And the prayers of those who thus ask from their heavenly Father who "knows," will be brief, simple, direct, expectant.

This, then, is the frame of mind and attitude of heart, that we should bring ourselves into during this period preparatory to prayer. In these all-important moments let us set our hearts upon sincerity, secrecy, simplicity, and serenity in prayer. Prayer will become more meaningful if the heart is sincere, more worshipful if the door is shut, more joyful if the language is simple, more wonderful if the mind is serene. This preparation for prayer need not be lengthy or complex, but it is necessary if our prayers are to be modeled upon the great pattern Prayer which our Lord introduces when He says, "After this manner therefore pray ye" (Matt. 6:9).

PATTERN FOR PRAYER

First, a word or two about the introductory phrase in Matthew 6:9a. The words "after this manner" mean (a) that our Lord meant this prayer to be a *method* of prayer; (b) He also meant it to be a *pattern* of prayer, since He offered it to the Twelve as a model prayer. The Lord's Prayer, therefore, should be for us both a method and a pattern of prayer. That is not to say, of course, that the form used here is the only legitimate one for Christians to use in prayer. The Lord's Prayer, in reality, sanctions all prayer, be it prescribed or unpremeditated so long as it is after the same pattern which is used in this prayer, and so long as it is used in the same spirit as that which prevails in this prayer, the spirit of liberty, trustfulness, and simplicity. In a word, this prayer is, so to speak, the prototype of all Christian prayer; at the same time allowing room for freedom, variety, and spontaneity.

The command "pray ye" in this introductory phrase in verse 9 ought also to be noted. Such a command implies that all the Lord's children are to be praying children. There are to be no dumb children in the heavenly Father's family. The tiniest babe in Christ, though not knowing how to pray, must learn *from the start* of the Christian life to lisp the words "our Father," and thus articulate itself in prayer, no matter how stumbling and inadequate the words used appear to be.

1. It requires very little insight to see, as has already been pointed out, that there are three constituent parts in this prayer. The first is invocation: "Our Father who art in heaven" (Matt. 6:9b). There are three things to ponder here.

(i) The One who is invoked in this prayer is a Father. There is a sense in which these simple but moving words, "our Father," when used of God in prayer, mark a new point of departure in religious devotion. It was Jesus who taught men the reality and the nature of the Fatherhood of God, and made it the foundation and essence of religious life. This is the very first time that the words are addressed to God in prayer, so far as the Bible is concerned. It is true that the Old Testament refers to God as Father (Deut. 33:6, Isa. 63:16, 64:8, and cf. Ps. 103:13), but only as the Father of Israel. Israel was God's son (Ex. 6:12), whom He had loved as His child (Jer. 31:9, Hos. 11:1); but it was only in Jesus Christ that God, in a unique sense, revealed Himself as Father. And this not in the sense that restricts His Fatherhood to His creatorship, but rather in the sense that in Jesus Christ He had revealed Himself as Savior and Redeemer; and for those who accept the saving grace of the God of redemption He is Father. And it is, of course, this "special Fatherhood of grace" that is in view in this invocation in the Lord's Prayer.

It is only those who are children of God through saving grace who can go on to pray, "Hallowed be thy name. Thy kingdom come. Thy will be done on earth." That is why this prayer is essentially a Christian prayer, the prayer of the Christian Church. All men have God as Father in the sense that He created them in His own image; but in another and unique sense God is the Father of the believer in Christ because the believer has been reconciled to God through the death of Christ. The Christian has a continual witness to that fact through the Holy Spirit whom the Father sends into the redeemed heart, and through whom the Father imparts to the believer His own divine nature, by virtue of which the believer is God's child, a member of Christ's Body, a citizen of God's kingdom. He it is who can pray this prayer in reality.

That is why it is apposite to remind ourselves, as Calvin teaches (Institutes, III, xx), that all prayer should be addressed to God only in the name of our Lord Jesus Christ. Now, while this is not explicit in this prayer, it is nevertheless implicit. It is implied tacitly in our addressing God as Father because it is only through Christ that one can come to know God as Father, and can use that sacred name in prayer. God ever waits to receive and bless those who come to Him through Jesus Christ. He sheds abroad in their hearts the Spirit of adoption who witnesses with the believers that they have been born of God, enables them to cry, "Abba! Father," and teaches them how to pray to their Father, and what to ask from their Father. Indeed, the more the Holy Spirit guides the Christian into the total truth about God as revealed in Jesus Christ, the more he comes to see that of all the names applied to God that of Father expresses His being and character in the fullest and truest sense.

(ii) The second point to notice in this invocation concerns those who invoke the divine Father: "*Our* Father." The gracious Fatherhood of God reminds all those who thus invoke Him as Father in prayer that they are brothers and sisters one of another. If I am a son or a daughter of God through grace, then, in virtue of that same saving grace I am a brother or a sister of every child of God begotten in Jesus Christ. And since the members of Christ's Body are so closely knit together none should pray exclusively for himself, but should, while showing due concern for his own needs, pray for others. Every time a Christian prays the Lord's Prayer he is reminded of the great world-wide family, of which Jesus Christ is the Head, and of which he (the believer) is a member and should, therefore, feel personally responsible for the welfare of his brothers and sisters in Christ. The question that Cain asked, "Am I my brother's keeper?" should be on the lips of a Christian only when an affirmative answer is implied.

How much more effective would have been the witness of the Church in the world, had she, to revert to Christ's High-Priestly Prayer in John 17, manifested that oneness for which her Lord prayed long ago; or, according to the simile in this Prayer in Matthew 6, had she remembered that all who form the Body of Christ are brothers and sisters, members of the same family of God who is the God and Father of our Lord Jesus Christ. We must increasingly act upon this dual relationship in which we as Christians stand toward our Father and toward each other as members of the one family in heaven and on earth which is named after the same Father, blessed for ever.

It is, therefore, brotherly love that should characterize the lives of all who call God their Father. In holding up holy hands in prayer toward the Father whose name we invoke, we should also stretch out helping hands to those in need. And this is a loving concern that should transcend all denominational, national, and social circles. It is a loving concern which in prayer should embrace the whole "household of faith" (Gal. 6:10). How many of us, who invoke "our Father" in prayer, try to enter into fellowship with, for example, our brothers and sisters in China in their fierce affliction, or with the lonely converts living amid fearful isolation in a hostile Muslim world, or with the missionaries who labor on year after year amid the unresponsive and fanatically opposed millions in the world of Islam? All that, and infinitely more, is involved in our addressing God as "our Father" in prayer.

(iii) The third point to notice in the invocation concerns the glory of the Father whom we invoke in prayer: "Our Father *who art in heaven.*" The phrase speaks of the Father's perfection of love and holiness, wisdom and power. Since "God is spirit," the phrase "in heaven" has, of course, no reference to a fixed geographical or special sphere. It must have reference rather to those realms that transcend our material existence; remembering, at the same time, that God is present with us in this time and space mode of existence.

"Our Father who art in heaven" means our Father who is the changeless One, the Almighty One who is without beginning or end. He is the Creator, Sustainer, Ruler of all, who inhabits eternity, and yet deigns to dwell with the lowly and contrite among the children of men. We should, in prayer, cultivate a high conception of God; a conception that agrees with the revelation of Himself in Jesus Christ, the only-begotten Son who is in the bosom of the Father. "His throne is in the heavens, and His kingdom ruleth over all"; we ought, therefore, ever to worship and adore Him with hearts aflame with love. This phrase, "who art in heaven," also reminds us that God is worshipped as Father by angels and archangels in glory, and by the spirits of just men made perfect.

What a transformation would be effected in our prayer life if we carried with us into our communion a high and a noble view of God, a Father who is infinitely near and infinitely transcendent, omnipotent yet personal, high and lofty, who dwells in the high and holy place, and yet dwells also with him who is contrite and humble. What preparation of heart would precede our prayers, what worship and adoration would characterize our prayers, what serenity of mind and spirit would breathe through our prayers, and how daring our prayers would become, if we really believed it was to such a Father in heaven that we were coming in prayer, a Father to whom nothing was impossible, to whom nothing was too hard. If our concept of God is small our prayers will be correspondingly meager; if our view of God is great our prayers will be correspondingly venturesome. We should cultivate, and carry about with us, a high and adequate conception of God. That will affect our prayers as nothing else will.

2. The second of the three constituent parts of the Lord's Prayer is petition. This second section of the prayer is made up of six petitions. The first three have reference to God — God's name, God's kingdom, and God's will; we shall consider each of these in turn.

(i) "Hallowed be thy name" (Matt. 6:9b). It is salutary to notice that the first thought in this fundamental pattern of all Christian prayer is not our wants or wishes, but the name of God. This is reflected in Jesus' own practice of prayer (John 12:28). It is worth while to remind ourselves once again of the importance of a name in Old Testament times. It was frequently a revelation of the character of the person who bore it. That is, in part, why the names of God are given such prominence in the Old Testament. Each was a fresh and a fuller revelation of the nature of God. One was a revelation of His might, another was the unveiling of His grace. One revealed something more of His wisdom, another of His holiness, another of His glory. In the New Testament God's name means God's nature as revealed in Jesus Christ; what God is in Himself, His being and attributes, as disclosed in Jesus Christ, and now known and confessed by the Church. The name of God, therefore, assumes an ever richer content for the Christian as the Holy Spirit teaches him; but here in the Lord's Prayer the particular name that God is asked to hallow is that of Father. That is the name God is to glorify, and cause to be revered among men.

This is a petition that still requires to be made in prayer because, more than ever, God's name is blasphemed and shamefully profaned. But what does the petition signify? "Hallowed be thy name" means, "Cause Thy name, Thy self-disclosure in Jesus Christ, O Father, to be revered and vindicated, and enable us to exalt and revere that same name by seeking to love, obey, honor and trust Thee with our whole heart." It also means, "Let Thy name be regarded as holy." The phrase to hallow or sanctify the name occurs twice in the Old Testament (Isa. 29:23, Ezek. 36:23); and to use it in prayer implies that the worshipper will have a profound awe for all that God has revealed of His nature and purpose in Jesus Christ.

To pray this petition sincerely means that one will endeavor to keep holy, and sanctify, in his own heart, the ineffable name of God. "Hallowed be thy name" means, "Enable me to worship Thee aright, by giving Thee the glory due unto Thee, by allowing my own mind and spirit to be penetrated with a due sense of Thine own perfection of grace, and holiness, and power, and a due sense of my own sinfulness and finiteness, that I may be humbled before Thee, and also a due sense of the wonder of Thy good gifts, such as Thy house, Thy Word, Thy works, Thy Church, the disclosure of Thyself in nature, reason, and conscience, as well as in the face of Jesus Christ." All this is implied in our asking God to hallow His name.

(ii) The second petition in the Prayer has reference to God's kingdom: "Thy kingdom come" (Matt. 6:10a). What is meant by the word "kingdom" in this petition? Through the Old Testament prophets, the Jewish hope of a Messianic kingdom had often come to expression, and now in our Lord's teaching it is given a central place; and so far as the nature of this kingdom is concerned it is seen to correspond to the nature of the King who rules over it, the one universal God, all loving, all holy, all powerful. There are at least three things we should keep in mind when thinking about the kingdom of God.

(a) The kingdom is a spiritual reality that is already present among men (Matt. 12:28, Luke 17:21). "Thy kingdom come" means, "May Thy rule enter the heart." Understood in terms of the holy rule of our Father-God in grace in the heart the kingdom of God is something that has already come. It is something that comes inwardly before it can come outwardly. To use a well-known New Testament simile, individual regeneration must precede social regeneration. As an individual spiritual reality, the kingdom of God comes when a man, born of the Holy Spirit, begins to deny himself, take up his cross daily, and follow Christ. The kingdom of God is within the man who, having been born of the Spirit, reckons himself to have died to sin, and endeavors daily, through the Spirit, to mortify the deeds of the body (Rom. 8:13), and have his fruit unto holiness (Gal. 5:22). From this point of view the petition "Thy kingdom come" will be answered when we begin with ourselves, and make sure that the kingdom is in our own hearts, and that we are in the kingdom. "Thy kingdom come" means, "Let righteousness triumph over unrighteousness," but that will be a sincere prayer only when we labor to let such a triumph manifest itself in our own lives. We will be really praying "Thy kingdom come" when truth triumphs over error in our own lives, grace over selfishness, holiness over sin, concord over disunity. It is, from this point of view, a prayer for our own growth in grace, and usefulness in the kingdom, for whose coming among men we pray and work.

(b) The coming of this kingdom to the individual is not an end in itself. Indeed, it is only the beginning. There is a corporate aspect of the kingdom of God in the New Testament. After we are in the kingdom individually, we must turn our eyes outward to the great world where evil spirit forces work to bring God's kingdom to nought. The kingdom of God, it must be understood, is not yet universally present in the sense that natural law and the moral law are universally present. It is a kingdom of grace, and the Christian, in fellowship with his brother believers in the Church, must pray and work for the coming of the kingdom of grace into the hearts of others, that the will of the King of grace may be done there too. When that takes place they, too, are brought into the kingdom. Men are saved individually, but they do not thereafter remain solitary units. Unitedly, Spirit-born men form a kingdom in which certain laws and principles of righteousness operate. We are members one of another in the kingdom of God, and it is our responsibility to evangelize the unsaved, that they, too, might become citizens of the kingdom in which God's Kingly rule of righteousness and holiness operates.

(c) But this kingdom is also a future event. Christ had already pronounced the kingdom to be at hand (Matt. 4:17). The conditions of entry into this kingdom He also made clear (John 3:5; Matt. 5:3, 10, 20). This kingdom is of such paramount importance that it is the supreme object of spiritual endeavor, and the supreme end of spiritual attainment (Matt. 6:33); but as a future event the kingdom of God includes features additional to these. The phrase "a new heaven, and a new earth" suggests that the kingdom includes the hope of eternal life, and that it will be an eternal reign of righteousness. The kingdom of God, therefore, is an eschatological event which has still to be ushered in when Jesus Christ comes again (Matt. 13:41f, 49f). It is at that point that Christ "will deliver up the kingdom to God, even the Father . . . that God may be all in all" (I Cor. 15: 24-28).

In the light of these considerations, then, it becomes clear that this petition, "Thy kingdom come," is no easy-going prayer that may be offered in an off-hand, slip-shod way. It is in fact a demanding prayer. It involves serious personal responsibilities. If it is offered sincerely it is a prayer that the King of the kingdom shall take complete possession of us, and exercise His Kingly rule over our lives; it is a prayer that through our Christ-dominated hearts He will gain an entrance into other lives; and it is a prayer that the day that still tarries will soon dawn when the same Kingly Lord Jesus will appear in glory on the clouds of heaven, to establish His kingdom by making the kingdom of this world His own. "Thy kingdom come" is a sham prayer unless it is offered by the man who loves not the world, neither the things that are in the world, and does to death through the Spirit the lust of the flesh and passions, and becomes a disciplined agent through whom the Holy Spirit can work in other lives.

(iii) The third petition has reference to God's will: "Thy will be done on earth, as it is in heaven" (Matt. 6:10b). This petition concerning the will of God might well be described as the key to an understanding of the whole of this wonderful prayer. This is because the Christian who offers this petition is praying that God will strengthen him with might by His Spirit in the inner man to enable him to unite his will with God's will, and to purpose steadfastly in his heart to do God's will in everything. In this sense this third petition is the peak to which all that precedes in the prayer leads, and it is the fountainhead from which all that follows flows.

This searching petition ought to destroy, once and for all, the widely held notion that prayer is an attempt to bend God's will to ours. That is a fallacy. The true purpose of prayer is to enable us to bring our wills into harmony with God's will. Clearly, then, this petition resembles the second one in that the prayer "Thy will be done" will be answered when we begin with ourselves; when we begin to deal with those things that prevent God's will being done in our lives.

But in what sense are we to understand the word "will" in this petition? When many Christians pray this prayer they do so in the same sense in which Jesus offered His prayer in Gethsemane: "Not my will, but thine be done" (Luke 22:42); and doubtless there is justification for so interpreting the petition. In praying this prayer they make a fresh submission of themselves to divine Providence in daily life. Certainly, God's will may involve the

Christian in suffering and sorrow; and when this happens the petition "Thy will be done" may be a request for the grace of "patience and long suffering with joyfulness." And, of course, when the petition has reference to the Christian's submission to the afflictions and trials that befall him in the providence of God, it is not to be offered in dumb resignation or sullen submission, but spontaneously and joyously, that the Father's purposes may be accomplished The finest commentary on the use of the petition in this sense is our Lord's use in Gethsemane (Matt. 26:42) of the very words that He teaches His disciples here to use in prayer. From this point of view the prayer is the spontaneous cooperation of our wills with that of God's will, whether it brings joy (Matt. 7:21, 12:50), or sorrow (Acts 21:14).

But there is a second significance attaching to this third petition. The qualifying phrase "on earth, as it is in heaven," gives the petition a far wider sweep and reach than mere acceptance of the inevitable, or submission to destiny, or to an eternal decree. The petition "Thy will be done" may signify that God's will is to be done in us that we may become active participators in its accomplishment; it may imply the desire that God's all-commanding will be done, and the desire to cooperate for its fulfillment. God works through means, and where He works among men His means are men, consecrated personalities, men of daring faith and venturesome obedience; and the men who pray sincerely are those who have caught something of the spirit of the angelic hosts who, being mighty in strength, fulfill God's commands and do His good pleasure, men whose meat and drink it is to do the will of God.

This third petition, then, involves inescapably a new act of obedience, not merely passive submission, every time it is offered, as, of course, does the second petition, "Thy kingdom come." To pray "Thy will be done" is sheer humbug unless it leads to a liberation from selfishness and self-centredness, and a corresponding self-committal to the will of God; just as the prayer "Thy kingdom come" is a sham prayer unless we allow the kingdom, and the King of the kingdom, to enter our hearts, and exercise His blessed authority there. And if to these two petitions we add the prayer, "Hallowed be thy name," and make it a point of ambition to hallow that sacred name in our own lives, we shall begin to understand just how searching are the demands that the sincere offering of such a prayer makes upon those who pray it.

(iv) The fourth petition is, "Give us this day our daily bread" (Matt. 6:11). Up to this point the Lord's Prayer has had its center in God — the person of God as the heavenly Father, the name of God, the kingdom of God, and the will of God. In verse 11 the prayer finds another center, namely, those who offer the prayer; it is to be understood, however, that everything in the prayer still has reference to God. We are encouraged to ask things for ourselves, but the motive that prompts the petitions must be that what is granted will be used to bring glory to God. Now, as there are three petitions in the Godward aspect of the prayer, centering around God's name, God's kingdom and God's will, so in the manward aspect there are three petitions, and these center around three perennial human needs — our need of bread, of forgiveness, and of victory. This fourth petition concerns the first of these very human matters, daily bread.

By including this petition in the prayer, our Lord is saying that we should ask our Father to supply us with the material necessities of life, which are here gathered up in one word, bread. Not only bread but clothing, shelter, money with which to buy these, health to enable us to earn the money, and all the other necessities as these arise day by day. To pray for "our daily bread" from our heavenly Father means that we acknowledge that it is upon Him that we depend to supply these necessities, that we exercise faith in Him to do so, and that we recognize that although these come to us in the providence of God through the labor of our hands and brains yet finally they come to us through the blessing and favor of God.

The Greek word *epiousios,* rendered "daily," occurs only here and in Luke 11:3. It should perhaps be rendered either "for the coming day," or "what is needful or sufficient"; and preferably the latter. The request is not for bread to cover many days' needs in advance, but for each day's needs as they come. The petition is for bread sufficient to meet present needs. It reminds man of his limitations, and of his dependence upon God, and, therefore, bids him cast his cares upon God. It curbs human greed and ambition. It is a request for bread, not luxuries; for enough to sustain us in life that we may be the instruments of God's will. In fact, the petition enforces the principle laid down in the Old Testament which controlled the gathering and use of the manna. In Exodus 16:14 the principle is stated, "morning by morning"; that is to say, a day's portion every day. The same principle in the divine economy occurs again in II

Kings 25:30: "Every day a portion, all the days of his life." This petition may also be related to the Christian's daily spiritual needs, understanding "bread" to symbolize Christ the living Bread, upon whom the soul feeds by faith.

The petition should curb among Christians all haste to enrich themselves. It also takes up Christ's warning against over-anxiety concerning temporal needs. It implies confidence in our heavenly Father that He who met our needs yesterday will not fail tomorrow. Be our station high or low in life, be our circumstances poor or comfortable, we are to pray, "Give us this day bread for our needs." If we live in the midst of plenty this should still be our daily prayer because it is an acknowledgment that abundance of material possessions is a curse if God's blessing does not accompany them. This petition means that our possessions have been apportioned to us by God, and that we use them only as He permits. How the Father's heart must rejoice when one of His children, though living in opulent circumstances, is still humble enough to pray sincerely, "Give us this day the bread that is needful."

(v) The fifth petition concerns another great human need, the need for forgiveness: "Forgive us our debts as we forgive our debtors" (Matt. 6:12). It is only to be expected that a sense of sinfulness will grow as we pray this prayer. In Matthew 7:11, God's children are said to be "evil"; and since their heavenly Father is "perfect" (Matt. 5:48), and wills their sanctification (I Thess. 4:7), they will increasingly become aware of their own moral imperfections, and realize the need for divine forgiveness.

There are two main points to notice in this fifth petition. (a) The word "debts" is not only an accurate rendering of the Greek word *opheilimata;* it is also an accurate description of the tragic significance of our sins. In classical Greek Matthew's word is used of ordinary debts, but here in the prayer it refers to moral debts which we incur with God when we sin. Even St. John's definition of sin, "sin is lawlessness" (I John 3:4), may be understood in terms of debt with God. In his *Commentary on the Johannine Epistles* Westcott shows how this works out in daily life. In dealing with this verse in John's first Epistle Westcott shows that in the providence of God each of us stands inescapably in a threefold relationship — with God, with oneself, and with others. Each of these relationships is conditioned by certain laws, laws which are divine, not human, in origin. They are laws which God has woven into the warp and woof of human nature in general, and of each personality in particular; and when we break these laws we come into the category described by John: "Every one that doeth sin doeth also lawlessness; and sin is lawlessness." Even sins against ourselves and our fellows are sins against God because they are committed against creatures created in the divine image; indeed, such sins are the equivalent of a denial of the Biblical doctrine of man. Every sin is a blow at the heart of God, and is part of the appalling debt that we incur with God. This is a debt that we cannot pay, and therefore we must either suffer the consequences, or have the debt forgiven; and here in the Lord's Prayer, Jesus Christ, whose death was to make forgiveness possible, teaches us to bend our proud hearts and humbly ask from God forgiveness of our debts: "Forgive us our debts."

(b) The second point in this petition is that the procuring of forgiveness from God is no easy matter. God's forgiveness is conditioned. If we wish to be forgiven we must be forgiving. No one who has not forgiven his enemy can really pray the Lord's Prayer, which is another reminder that this is a specifically Christian prayer. The better reading of the petition is, "Forgive us our debts, as we also *have* forgiven our debtors." That is to say, our forgiving our debtors is a completed act before we begin to pray God to forgive us: not, of course, that we can forgive the guilt involved in the wrong another has done us; only God can forgive that.

And we forgive by casting forth from our hearts all rancor and spite which a rankling sense of injury engenders: all desire to be avenged of our enemies; the nursing of a sense of wrong by keeping it ever green in the memory. It has already been suggested that as one gives oneself increasingly to prayer, a growing awareness of personal sinfulness will begin to possess the heart; but it should be remembered that a necessary corollary to this increasing sense of sinfulness will be a more lenient view of the shortcomings of others. To come to the Father for forgiveness for ourselves, and at the same time keep the fires of active resentment or passive illwill burning against "our debtors," is a mockery.

Many Christians have never faced the fact that in our Lord's doctrine of prayer, and, indeed, in His teaching generally, there is a close moral connection between divine and human forgiveness (cf. Mark 11:25f., Luke 6:37, Matt. 18:23-25). So insistent is our Lord on this point that there is added an explanatory remark on the fifth petition after He has completed the prayer

(Matt. 6:14f.). The ground upon which the claim for divine forgiveness is made is our having already forgiven our debtors. This, of course, is not the whole ground upon which the plea for forgiveness is made. Divine remission of sins is conditioned by a right attitude of heart toward God; an attitude that manifests itself in repentance (Luke 24:47), confession (I John 1:9), and faith (Matt. 9:2); but this attitude will include a right disposition toward our debtors.

In insisting upon this in prayer Jesus is simply emphasizing a point already driven home in the previous part of the Sermon on the Mount, where reconciliation with God is conditioned by reconciliation with men (cf. 5:23f., 43-48). This is an application of the Golden Rule: "Whatever ye would that men should do unto you, even so do ye also unto them" (Matt. 7:12). The same rule is enforced with great power in the parable of the Unmerciful Servant (Matt. 18:21-25); but far from this "condition" limiting divine forgiveness, it widens its scope and strengthens its efficacy. The "condition" does not mean that we bring God under an obligation to forgive us when we "forgive our debtors," nor that we, by forgiving others, merit forgiveness from God; but it does mean that when we forgive our debtors we receive the assurance that God forgives our debts. In the region of free grace there is a law of retribution in operation. If we do not forgive, we shall not be forgiven.

If we really took seriously this undoubted connection between divine and human forgiveness, how revolutionary would this fifth petition become! What a revolution it would effect in all the ramifications of our human relations. The bitternesses and the jealousies and the grudges that have lain like a black frost for years across some of our relationships would give way to the sunshine of God's love that is supposed to have been shed abroad in our hearts by the Holy Spirit. Do we really want to be forgiven by God? First, then, let us be reconciled with our brother.

(vi) The sixth petition concerns our temptations: "Lead us [or bring us] not into temptation, but deliver us from evil [or the evil one]" (Matt. 6:13a). "Lead us" is used in the sense of allowing us to be brought into circumstances where we are tested and tried. What God allows is spoken of as if it were an act of God; hence the petition, "Lead us not . . . . but deliver us." There are three or four matters that should engage our attention here.

(a) There is for many Christians a problem in this petition, the solution of which is in a correct understanding of the word "temptation." What is meant by temptation in this prayer: So far as the origin of temptation is concerned there are three observations to make. (i) Temptation may originate in those evil passions and desires which spring from our fallen human nature. In this sense, temptation may be understood in terms of assaults of the evil one. In this connection James 1:3 is significant. God does not tempt us to evil. The origin of this kind of temptation, as James goes on to point out in 1:14f., is in our evil concupiscence and lusts, which the evil one may stir up, or we ourselves may deliberately incite, and so create temptation to sin. (ii) Temptation may emanate from those things which, although not evil in themselves, may, if allowed to master us, bring us into bondage that is sinful. (iii) Temptation may originate in the hard experiences of life; experiences in the shape of trials and sorrows, physical, moral, and spiritual, by which God desires to purify and refine; but which may engender despair in our minds, or doubts concerning God's love and power, or even rebellion against God's providential dealings; rebellion that leads to prayerlessness, neglect of the Word, and remissness in service for Christ.

Clearly, then, our understanding of this petition will be determined by the sense in which we take the word "temptation." We may feel justified in dividing the whole phrase into two distinct petitions. For example, if the words "deliver us from evil" be taken as a prayer to have one's heart delivered from evil, then it will form a request that is completely separate from the preceding one, "Lead us not into temptation." The former phrase will become the seventh petition, instead of the closing part of the sixth, and will assume a significance that goes far beyond the sense in which the two phrases are usually taken. This would agree well with the passages in the Sermon on the Mount in which Christ refers to the Christian's aspirations after personal holiness.

(b) If, however, the whole phrase is offered as a single petition, the word temptation may be understood to imply simply a test or trial that has no moral significance, either good or bad, attaching to it. For example, in Genesis 22:1, "God did prove Abraham," but only in order to test the strength of his faith. Again, in John 6:6, "This he [Jesus] said to prove [or test] him [Philip]." These were not evil but righteous trials; tests that sifted or winnowed; tests of moral principles, but not solicitations to evil. This, of course, brings the two phrases of the petition together to form one request; and this is doubtless the sense in which the word temptation should be understood in this verse. The petition "deliver us" does not imply cowardice or selfishness; it is an acknowledgment of humility, of dependence upon God, and is a request that He bring us not into situations where we are tested beyond endurance.

There is, therefore, no conflict between Matthew 6:13, and James 1:13, because James has in mind solicitation to evil, whereas in the Lord's Prayer it is a question of the divine providences which bring us into situations where temptations may arise; but if that happens, God will intervene to provide a way of escape (I Cor. 10:13). However, the prayer "Bring us not into temptation" may well have to be qualified on occasion, as was Jesus' request in Gethsemane: "Nevertheless, not my will, but thine be done." When we pray, "Bring us not into trial," we may have to add, "But if it please Thee to test us, in that hour 'deliver us from evil,' that the evil one may not triumph over us."

If the question, Why pray for deliverance from temptation? be raised, it may be observed (as Paul implies in I Cor. 10:13) that the issue of anyone temptation is always in doubt. Then, again, the Christian naturally shrinks from testing. Therefore, although much good comes of trial, it is always appropriate for the Christian to pray, "Bring me not into trial, but deliver me out of the power of the evil one." In any case, such a prayer reminds us that the Lord is not the tempter but the Deliverer. It also leads us to confess consciously, voluntarily, submissively, and prayerfully that we are wholly dependent upon Him. It reminds us, too, that the Christian doctrine of temptation preserves both the believer's freedom and his dependence upon God.

(c) The third point that this petition makes clear is that we do not reach a stage where temptation or trial disappears. We are, however, to "count it all joy . . . when [we] fall into manifold temptations" (James 1:2), because they may become a means of grace to us. Exemption from testing and sifting would remove all the tang and verve from the Christian life. Without trial the Christian life would become a supine affair. We require constantly to be stimulated, and exhilarated, and urged to press on. Even the Lord learned obedience by the things that He suffered (Heb. 5:8).

(d) And in the fourth place, we should remember that these trials may become a rock of offense, and a stone of stumbling to us. A sudden gust of temptation, and a whole lifetime of shining honor may disappear in a welter of shame. Here it is apposite to recall the Lord's word to the Apostles in Gethsemane. There they were encouraged to watch and pray lest they enter into temptation. They eventually did fall into temptation, but the temptation was self-incurred, because they failed to watch and pray; they exercised their sinful self-dependence, which lulled them into a feeling of false security.

What, then, must Christians do? Let him that thinketh he standeth do two things: let him take heed to himself, and let him pray. Our very privileges and opportunities become temptations; "a chance to rise is a chance to fall." The Christ who prayed for Peter that his faith fail not when Satan was sifting him like wheat (Luke 22:31f.), is the Christ who prays for us now, as He prayed for us in His High-Priestly Prayer. In that prayer, it will be remembered, Christ does not ask the Father to take the Apostles from the world, but to keep them from the evil one. So with us. On the one hand, it is the will of the Father that we should be exposed to trial and testing in the world; on the other hand, it is the Father's will, and desire, to keep us unspotted from the world in the hour of temptation. This keeping power is in Jesus Christ who was tempted as we are, sin excluded. That power is available for us, but it has to be appropriated by us by faith; and it is the indwelling Holy Spirit who communicates Christ's power to us, by strengthening us with might in the inner man. We must, therefore, constantly make this petition ours: "Bring us not into trial, but deliver us from the evil one, we having no delivering strength in ourselves."

3. The third main element in the Lord's Prayer, as it now stands in Matthew's Gospel, is doxology. It is certain, however, that this was not a part of the original prayer. All the ancient authorities omit it. But although it is a liturgical ending, we shall include it for comment, for the sake of completeness.

The prayer began with God, and at its close it returns to God. In the doxology there is more than a hint of the triune name of God, Father, Son and Holy Spirit. "Thine is the kingdom" directs our thoughts to God the Son who rules over this kingdom; "Thine is the power" directs our thoughts to God the Holy Spirit, by whose power the Son's kingdom is extended throughout the world; "Thine is the glory" directs our thoughts to God the Father, whose glory has shone in the face of Jesus Christ.

In the doxology there are three great declarations of Christian faith (i) "Thine is the kingdom." Faith's petition, "Thy kingdom come," has become faith's affirmation, "Thine is the kingdom." So certain is it that the King of kings will deliver up the kingdom to the Father, and put down all rule, authority, and power, and subdue all things unto Himself, that the faith that prays, "Thy kingdom come," is the faith that affirms, "Thine is the kingdom." (ii) "Thine is the power." Power here may be the power of the Holy Spirit who works incessantly to advance the Son's glorious kingdom. In this phrase power is spiritual and moral dynamic, not physical force, that works to establish Christ's kingdom of holiness and peace. It is an inward spiritual dynamic that establishes Christ's Kingly rule in the heart by bringing all things into subjection to Christ. That is why our witness to the Lord Jesus, and our preaching, must be "in demonstration of the Spirit and power." (iii) "Thine is the glory." Glory here means reputation, esteem deriving from excellence of character, and power of action. Glory is here ascribed to the Father because He has gotten Himself glory in the Church through His wondrous acts of redemption in Christ Jesus. He has triumphed gloriously. As the psalmist exclaims: "God is gone up with a shout . . . God is the King over all the earth . . . God reigneth over the nations: God sitteth upon his holy throne . . . He is greatly exalted" (47:5-9).

To this threefold declaration, "Thine is the kingdom," "Thine is the power," "Thine is the glory," every Christian heart answers, "Amen!" That is to say, truly, verily, surely. "Amen" is our assent to this declaration; it is at the same time, our assent to the desires expressed in the preceding petitions. "Amen" means, "This is the confidence that we have in Him, that if we ask anything according to his will, he heareth us." What we ask, and declare, in this prayer, Christ Himself has taught us to ask and declare: "Amen," therefore, is faith's assurance that "we have the petitions which we have asked of Him" (I John 5: 15).

The Lord's Prayer starts with God our heavenly Father, and is concerned with His name, His kingdom, and His will; it now ends with God and is concerned with His kingdom, His power and His glory. The prayer does not ignore man's daily needs, man's sins, man's trials; but these do not predominate. Its primary concerns are God's glory, God's kingdom, God's will, God's power, God's love, God's sovereignty, God's wisdom; and as we murmur, "Lord, teach us to pray," the Master still replies, "After *this manner*, pray ye."

PAUSE AFTER PRAYER

The two verses that follow the Lord's Prayer are unaccountably neglected in many commentaries. The tendency is to dismiss them nonchalantly as an unimportant appendage to the prayer. From the point of view of context and content, however, they are significant.

1. The context. The context suggests that verses 14 and 15 are closely related to the prayer that precedes. They have reference to that part of the prayer that concerns both our need of God's forgiveness, and the conditions upon which that forgiveness is mediated to us (see pp. 16f., 96f.). In this brief appendix to the prayer Jesus returns to emphasize that part of the prayer that concerns the application of the law of love in Christian practice. Not only does He emphasize it, He *enforces* it in the most solemn manner. The assurance of God's love in terms of forgiveness is related to our forgiving the trespasses of those who trespass against us. Because, then, these two verses come immediately after, and arise out of, the prayer, they may be used to remind us of the importance of a brief period of meditation after prayer. They suggest the necessity for quiet reflection and spiritual recollection following prayer, for contemplation of what we have been doing, thinking, asking, confessing, resolving, vowing, in prayer.

2. The content. To those who delight to linger in the Father's presence for a few moments after prayer, Matthew 6:14-15 suggests three subjects for reflection.

(i) The Holiness of God. There are three aspects of transgression hinted at in these two verses: our own transgressions, men's transgressions against us, our transgression and theirs against God. Now, the holiness of God is outraged by a man's sins, whether they be committed against the Lord or against a man's fellows; and it is this outrage against God's holiness that makes God's forgiveness *necessary*. A pause for reflection after prayer on these truths will impart new insights into sin, into the havoc it works in a man's relations with his fellows and with God, into the reality of God's holiness, into the necessity to flee from unrighteousness and to cleave unto holiness as we pray the Lord's Prayer.

(ii) The Grace of God. Because God is holy He must take account of sin and deal with the sinner. He can deal with the sinner in judgment and lay upon him the punishment which his violation of the holiness of God incurs; or He can deal with the

sinner in grace. Here, then, is another great subject for reflection after prayer; as the outrage against God's holiness makes
God's forgiveness necessary, the grace of God makes His forgiveness *possible*.

(iii) The Justice of God. This is another great subject for
reflection during the pause after prayer. The holiness of God
standing over against the sinfulness of man makes divine forgiveness necessary; the grace of God makes divine forgiveness
possible; the justice of God makes forgiveness *conditioned*. The
justice of God takes account of sins committed by men against
men; the forgiveness of God which is mediated to men in prayer
is, therefore, morally conditioned, and to that extent not easy
to obtain. Divine forgiveness of our sin is related to our forgiving sins committed against us; and it is worth while to recall
that the best reading of Matthew 6:12 is: "And forgive us our
debts as we have forgiven our debtors." Our forgiving a man's
sins against us is an accomplished fact before God forgives us.
This third subject for meditation after prayer reminds us that
we who have been dealt with by God on the ground of grace,
must deal with our fellows on the same ground. Standing in
grace we must become gracious; having been justified, we must
become just; having been declared righteous, we must become
righteous; having obtained mercy from God, we must become
merciful; having been loved by God we must love our fellows.

This appendix to the Lord's Prayer, then, points the way out
of a serious weakness in our devotional life. Verses 5 to 8 remind
us of the necessity of preparing our hearts, with the aid of the
Holy Spirit, before we engage in the highest pursuit upon which
the human spirit can enter; but correspondingly, it is unseemly
to rush precipitately from God's presence without pausing for
a few moments for inward recollection and reflection. As this
dual habit is established, our devotional life will be enriched
at two points: as we go down from the secret place to the market
place the Spirit will make us more gracious in disposition; the
fragrance of secret communion will be carried down into the common ways of life; and men will take knowledge of us that we
have been with Jesus (Acts 6:13).

CHAPTER FIVE

A MERCIFUL AND FAITHFUL HIGH PRIEST

THE SUBJECT of this chapter is the High-Priestly ministry that Christ the Lord of glory has been fulfilling since His Ascension, and its significance for us today. Let us make a few preliminary observations by way of introduction.

(i) It is significant that the disciples returned to Jerusalem "with great joy" (Luke 24:52), after the Lord had lifted up His hands in benediction upon them (v. 50), and had been taken up from them into heaven (Acts 1:9). Why "with great joy," and not with heavy hearts, since this was the final parting from their Lord? Because of their conviction that the Redeemer had been "carried up into heaven" (Luke 24:51), and was now at "the right hand of the throne of the Majesty in the heavens" (Heb. 8:1).

(ii) But when the Father exalted the Son to His right hand (Acts 5:31), Jesus Christ did not enter merely into a state of perfect rest from the pain, and sorrow, and opposition experienced in His Incarnation. When an earthly king sits down on his throne he does not enter into a state of idleness. He assumes high responsibility. He takes up an arduous task of supreme importance. So with our Lord. He has been fulfilling a specific ministry from the moment the Father, after having highly exalted Him (Phil. 2:9), and "crowned him with glory and honor" (Heb. 2:9), made Him, that is to say, caused Him to be recognized as both Lord and Christ (Acts 2:36).

(iii) But what is this ministry in which the Lord of Glory has been engaged? Speaking for the moment in very general terms, Christ, in His heavenly life, has continued the work He initiated on earth. Having obtained eternal redemption for men, He now applies it to men. James Denney, in His *Studies in Theology* (p. 154), reminds us that Christianity depends almost as much on what Christ is, and does, now at this present moment, as on what He was, and did, on earth. The Lord belongs not only to the past, but also to the present and the future (Heb. 8:8). Still following Denney, Jesus Christ is the Almighty, the ever-present King of grace; we must learn, therefore, to put all

Christ ever was, all He ever did, all He ever suffered, into the present tense. He is now present in the grace of His earthly life and death, and in the omnipotence of His power to save. To lose sight of Christ exalted forever is to lose the consciousness of His presence, His power, and His peace in our hearts, and to lose the secret of victorious living. It is this Lord Jesus Christ who, from the throne, sends His Holy Spirit upon the Church, and exalts the Church on earth to sit with Him in the heavenlies, and gives her access to all the spiritual blessings that are in Him, and so enables her to live in the power of His own victorious life.

(iv) This reminds us of a peril to which the Church is constantly exposed. The danger is so to overemphasize the work Christ wrought in the past, in His Incarnation and redemptive death, that she either forgets, or fails to evaluate adequately, the work which He now accomplishes from the throne in glory. The Church must hold together in her thinking both Jesus the Carpenter of Nazareth and Christ the Lord of Glory. Since there is no conflict between these two views of our Lord in the New Testament, there should be no sense of conflict concerning them in the theological thinking of the Church.

A study of Christ's High-Priestly ministry will combine the wonderful words and deeds of Jesus Christ in the humility of His Incarnation, and the emancipating, quickening, saving work of the same Jesus Christ who now lives and reigns in highest heaven. In the Priestly ministry of Christ Galilee is not the antithesis of the heavenlies. In that ministry they form a synthesis. To regard Jesus of Nazareth as antithetical to Christ of glory is to do less than justice to the Person of Christ. It is to deny the New Testament conviction that Christ's present exaltation in glory presupposes His pre-existence, as well as His Incarnation, His sinless life, His atoning death and victorious resurrection. The exaltation of the Lord of Glory involves everything else that concerns Christ, and must, therefore, determine the very form and spirit of the Church's distinctive faith, experience and practice.

The Christ of the New Testament is the risen, ascended Lord. When Paul preached "Christ crucified" (I Cor. 1:23), he meant Jesus of Nazareth who died for our sins in the past, and Christ now exalted in heavenly places. The Lamb who had been slain is now standing in the midst of the throne, and to Him all power in heaven and earth has been given. The symbol of faith and worship in the New Testament is not a crucifix. Christ is no longer on the Cross but on the Throne. Naturally, then, the New Testament contains not "a single word of despondency or gloom. It is the most buoyant, exhilarating, and joyful book in the world" (James Denney). To recapture the New Testament's dynamic, we need to regain an awareness of the Lord's exaltation to the Throne. It is high time we recaptured the New Testament's unshakable and unassailable faith "in the reign of Christ in grace." As we proceed it will become clear that our glorified Lord's present ministry in the heavenlies has particular relevance to His practice and doctrine of prayer.

1. Before considering the nature of our Lord's High Priesthood in glory it may be well to notice its practical significance for the Christian today. This is well brought out by the late Griffith Thomas in his article entitled "Priest" in Hastings' *Dictionary of Christ and the Gospels*. This is quite the best summary of this subject known to the writer, and his debt to it is apparent at several points.

(i) It is significant that in the New Testament our ascended Lord's High-Priestly work is dealt with only in the Epistle to the Hebrews. Why is this? The reason is probably to be found in the situation which occasioned the Letter. It was written, we may assume, to Christians of long standing since the writer implies that they themselves should have become teachers (5:12), and since those who had led them to Christ were now dead (13:7). But after having been so long enlightened they had steadily declined in spiritual life. They again needed someone to teach them the elementary principles of the faith (5:12-14). Because they were not going on to maturity in Christian knowledge they were in danger of spiritual degeneracy (5:12), and spiritually apostasy (6:9, 10:35). The author, therefore, was earnestly solicitous for them (6:11), and urged them not to cast away their confidence (10:35). They had been subjected to persecution and reproach, and to help them bear this "reproach of Christ," the writer reminds them, not only that Christ Himself had suffered (12:2), but also that they now have a great High Priest, Jesus the Son of God, who helps them in time of need (4:14-16, 5:1-5, 12:2-4). Apparently the author felt that to save those Hebrew Christians from spiritual suicide it was necessary to give them a fresh understanding of the High Priesthood of the reigning Lord.

(ii) And this is where the practical significance of this same great truth resides for us today. An understanding of Christ's present ministry in glory as our High Priest is imperative to steadfastness in faith, to constant growth in grace, and to assurance of our standing in Christ. In the measure in which the Holy Spirit gives us new insights into the High Priesthood of Christ, and in the measure in which we, by faith and obedience, lay hold of these new insights, we shall grow in grace, remain firmly rooted in Christ, and go on to Christian maturity. The Christian's full growth is growth or maturity in knowledge of Christ. A growing apprehension of Jesus Christ, therefore, and new insights into the total meaning of Christ, are essential to Christian development. It is essential to know Him as Savior; it is also essential to know and to participate in that free access to the Father's presence through the same Savior who is our High Priest. In that access we find peace, power, freedom from fear, and joy. Christians must enter into the experience of the Redeemer's Priesthood; otherwise they are ignorant of one of the essential conditions of spiritual growth and maturity. Herein, then, lies the practical value of our subject, and its necessity for faith. If Christians wish to "go on to perfection" (6:1) and to make certain that they will not "fall away" (6:6) or "shrink back" (10:39), they must "draw near" to God, often and regularly, through their merciful and faithful High Priest, Jesus the exalted Lord.

2. Our next concern is to inquire into the nature of the High Priesthood of Jesus Christ. It will be useful to ask at the outset, What is it that makes a priestly ministry necessary at all? Priesthood is essential because of the covenant relation between God and His people. It was because Israel was in covenant relation with God that a priesthood was necessary for them. They required someone to minister to them and represent them. To this extent priesthood was the cement of the community in Israel (7:11). Now three things are essential to any priestly ministry: a sanctuary where God is, a way of access into the sanctuary, and a sacrifice to offer for acceptance with God. These were the essentials of priestly service under the old covenant, and they are still necessary under the new.

It is also true, of course, that the priest's importance was determined by his "order"; and by "order" the author of Hebrews means the priest's person, what he was in himself. This was important because it determined the kind of sacrifice he would offer, the type of sanctuary in which he would offer the sacrifice, and the nature of his approach to God. By themselves the

sacrifice, the sanctuary, and the access were important, because
upon them depended the maintenance of the covenant relation;
but behind the priest's ministry there was something of even
more fundamental importance — the priest's own person or
"order." Upon that everything depended.

What, then, was the nature of Christ's Priesthood? To what
"order" did He belong? His Priesthood is said to be after the
order of Melchizedek, the significance of whose priesthood was
determined by what he was in himself. Now all that we know of
the history of Melchizedek is in Genesis 14:18-20. The only other
Old Testament reference to him is in Psalm 110:4. Hebrews 5
is an interpretation of these two passages. We have space to
mention only two points.

(i) In Genesis 14:18, it is emphasized that Melchizedek was
a king, that his name means king of righteousness, and that he
was king of Salem, that is to say, king of peace. Thus he
typified "Jehovah our righteousness" (Jer. 23:6), and "the Prince
of Peace" (Isa. 9:6). Now it is both the kingly nature of
Melchizedek, and his kingly attributes of righteousness and
peace, that are emphasized in Hebrews 7:2. Righteousness is
that which makes a relation with God possible, and peace is the
result of the relation. It was natural, therefore, that later writers
in Scripture should see in Melchizedek a type of the coming
Messiah whose kingdom would be one of righteousness and
peace. But, of course, Melchizedek was more than a king. In
him kingship and priesthood were united (cf. Zech. 6:13), and
as a kingly priest he typified Christ the royal Priest.

(ii) In the opinion of the writer of Hebrews, however, the
most wonderful thing about Melchizedek has not yet been told.
Although he exercised priestly functions he belonged to no
priestly family. The failure of Genesis to furnish us with a
record of his ancestry signifies that Melchizedek's priesthood was
inherent in, and was dependent upon, his own person, and upon
nothing else. His priesthood was determined by what he was in
his own person.

The Old Testament is also silent, however, concerning the
actual moment of his entering the priesthood, and of his retirement from it. This signifies that he was a priest who, in his own
person, fulfills forever all priestly functions. He thus typifies a
priesthood received from no ancestors, and transmitted to no
descendants. Now in Hebrews 7:3 this symbolizes the endless
duration of our Lord's Priesthood, and crystalizes the great

difference between the Melchizedek and the Aaronic priesthoods.

For the members of the latter priesthood, everything depended upon their belonging to a certain family. They had to produce their genealogies and registers (Ezra 2:4f, Neh. 7:63f), in order to prove the purity of their descent on both sides. The question which a Jew, who was being urged to trust the priestly mediation of Jesus Christ, would ask would be, "What are His credentials?" The Christian, in reply, would be forced to accede that Christ came forth from a tribe that had nothing to do with priesthood. Even the claim that He was a direct descendant of the royal Davidic line would, in the opinion of the Jew, automatically eliminate Him from the priestly office. The author of Hebrews, however, answers these objections by pointing out that the Old Testament makes reference to a priest who was greater than Aaron, and who is, therefore, a more worthy type of the Messiah. His greatness lay in his being king as well as priest, and in his being the one and only priest of his order.

3. We now must consider Aaron's priesthood in relation to Jesus Christ's Priesthood. It is principally in chapters 5 and 7 of the Epistle to the Hebrews that a comparison is made between the two priesthoods, a comparison that throws light on the nature of the Lord's priestly work.

(i) The office for which every Aaronic high priest was appointed for men was that of offering both "gifts and sacrifices for sins" (5:1, 8:3). The phrase covers all kinds of offerings. Sin must not be allowed to daunt the sinner from using the mediatory ministry of the high priest, since there would be neither priesthood nor sacrifice were there no sin. To those who sinned inadvertently, or through frailty (Lev. 4:2, 13), or willfully when seized with sudden passion or temptation (Lev. 5:1, 19:20-22), these sacrifices spoke pardon.

(ii) In order to perform this ministry well it was required that the high priest be sympathetic towards the ignorant and the erring (5:2-3) on whose behalf he ministered. He had to understand their needs, and feel leniently toward them. It was necessary, therefore, that the high priest be taken from among men because he, being himself compassed with infirmity and weakness, would deal gently with others. This compassion expressed itself in the offering of sacrifices for sins.

(iii) The Aaronic high priest could not assume his exalted office on his own initiative. Arrogance would have marked the exercise of the high priesthood of a man who had assumed the office out of personal assumption, or whim, or caprice. He had to be called of God (5:4). So Aaron himself (Ex. 28:1). The consciousness of divine call would tend to humility. This necessity of divine call is prominent in the Old Testament (Num. 3:10, 16:40, II Chron. 26:18-21; cf. I Kings 12:31). It ensured that those whom God called would have the suitable qualifications for priesthood.

(iv) The author of the Epistle to the Hebrews goes on to show in 5:5-10 that these very qualities had been manifested in the divine High Priest, Jesus Christ. (a) He, too, had been appointed to His High-Priestly ministry by His Father's command (5:5-6). But whereas appointment to the high priesthood had been an "honor" for Aaron, for Christ it had been "glory" (cf. 2:9, 3:3). It was glory for Him because He was appointed when He ascended to the Father's right hand. When the Father said, "Thou art my Son," He glorified Christ as Priest (Ps. 2:7, 110:4, Heb. 1:5). (b) As to character, Jesus Christ was also compassionate; but Hebrews is concerned to emphasize His obedience (5:7-8). The Lord's obedience was maintained in the face of mounting demands upon it, but these demands only led Him to enter more deeply into the nature and meaning of obedience (cf. Matt. 26: 39 and 41). He was obedient even unto death (10:5-10, Phil. 2:8); but it was along this pathway of implicit obedience to the Father's will that He learned how to succor the sorely tempted. (c) He fulfilled the office of High Priest when He became the Author of eternal salvation (5:9-10). The perfection spoken of here concerns the Lord's being equipped with every qualification to become the Originator of eternal salvation by the sacrifice of Himself, and a High Priest forever. When He was thus perfected He ascended up on high and appeared in the heavenly sanctuary, at which moment the Father saluted Him as a High Priest.

4. Did, then, these similarities with Aaron's priesthood make Christ's Priesthood after the order of the Aaronic priesthood? Quite the contrary. The writer of Hebrews shows that although Jesus fulfilled the requirements laid down by the Aaronic priesthood, He did not thereby become a Priest after Aaron's order. His Priesthood was after the order of Melchizedek and was, therefore, infinitely superior to that of Aaron. Christ's superiority both in order and priesthood becomes apparent when compared with the other features that characterized Aaron's. Aaron was a mortal man, subject to infirmity (7:28). The sanctuary in which Aaron

fulfilled his priesthood (9:7) belonged to this world (9:1). The plan of this sanctuary showed clearly that the way to God was barred (9:7). And the very ministry which he exercised was limited in that it was powerless to reach the conscience (9:9), or take away sin (10:2f). But after having said all that, the real superiority of Jesus Christ's Priesthood has still not been mentioned. Wherein did it really lie?

(i) It lay in the infinite superiority of His Person. Aaron was not a royal person, Christ was. Aaron was not an abiding person, "by reason of death"; Christ is eternal. Aaron had many successors, Christ was unique; and He was unique because He was made a Priest after the power of an indissoluble life (7:16). This life was endless, not only because Jesus was the pre-existent Son of God, but also because it was the life of the same eternal Son Incarnate in the flesh, whose life rose above death when for a moment it was subjected to death. The Prince of Life (Acts 3:15), having conquered death by dying, rose in triumph, and in the power of that endless or indissoluble life He entered upon His eternal High-priesthood when He entered the sanctuary on high.

(ii) And being infinitely superior in Person, Jesus Christ the great High Priest was infinitely superior in function; and this in three respects. (a) His covenant was better than Aaron's (8:7-13); better in that it was spiritual, not legal and temporal. The most serious fault in the old covenant was that it had no way of ensuring that men would keep it (cf. Gal. 3:21). It could not, therefore, effect the purpose for which it had been established; although, of course, the nature of the men who lived under it contributed to its ineffectiveness. By contrast, the new covenant (Jer. 31:31, Heb. 8:7-13), because it was written on the heart (8:10), would ensure obedience on the part of those who lived under it, would be universally known (8:11), and would ensure complete forgiveness of sins (8:12). In a word, the difference between the old covenant and the new was the difference between spirituality and legalism (cf. Ezek. 36:26-29). The new covenant is the covenant of the Holy Spirit, the Spirit who anoints, teaches, and empowers the forgiven, and enables them to serve God with unburdened conscience (9:14), and from the heart (10:22).

(b) Christ's sanctuary was better than Aaron's (8:1-6; 9:1-5, 11). It was heavenly, not earthly. It was the true sanctuary of which the earthly was merely a copy (8:3-5). And it was the true one because it is eternal and genuine; the earthly tabernacle being only a sketch of it. It may be worth while to point out that the word "tabernacle" includes all of the place where the priestly ministry was performed; the term "sanctuary," on the other hand, probably corresponds to the Holy of Holies, in which sanctuary Jesus Christ is now the ministering High Priest (9: 11-12).

(c) Christ's sacrifice was better than Aaron's (9:11-18). It was better in that it was a reality, not a symbol. And being a real sacrifice, it obtained eternal redemption (9:12). It is real and, therefore, works effectively with the conscience (9:14), it speaks of a final putting away of sin and thus brings to an end all sacrifice for sin (10:11-12), and through this sacrifice Christ perfects them that are sanctified (10:14).

(iii) Jesus Christ was also superior in His order. The superiority of Christ's order of Priesthood lay in its being forever. This eternal quality sealed and guaranteed the finality of Christ's High-Priestly ministry and the new covenant. But, as has already been noticed, the superiority of Jesus Christ's order really resided in the superiority of His Person (7:6). He was the Son of God, and His life was indissoluble.

(iv) The tribe to which Christ belonged, that of royal Judah, was superior to that of Aaron, the tribe of Levi (7:14). The fact that our Lord came forth from Judah (Gen. 49:10, Isa. 11:1, Luke 3:33, Rev. 5:5) and not Levi was profoundly significant for the writer of Hebrews. Jesus' coming forth from Judah and not Levi altered the Law (7:12), and proclaimed that priesthood was passing from Levi to Judah. It was also significant for Christ's order. He could not possibly be of Aaron's order because He was not of Aaron's tribe; but the real reason was that He was of the order of Melchizedek.

(v) Christ's call to His Priesthood was superior to that of Aaron's. The Father's call to the Son was superior because in it the Father bound Himself by an oath (7:21), whereas God's call to Aaron to his priesthood was without an oath. The significance of the oath was that it introduced something that was unchangeable. God's call to Aaron to occupy the office of high priest was without an oath and his priesthood was therefore temporary (7:23), as was also the covenant under which he ministered. Conversely, since Christ's call to His High Priesthood was confirmed by an oath, the new covenant is eternal. Christ the eternal Priest became surety of the eternal covenant. And now that He is Priest forever He enables men to draw near to God (7:18-19,

10:19); and having brought them nigh to God He is able to save them to the uttermost, or completely (7:23-25).

(5) Perhaps a little more should be said concerning the relationship between our Lord's High Priesthood and His Person. Here it should be recalled that by "order," whether of Melchizedek or of Levi, the author of Hebrews means the priest's person, what he is in himself. In chapter 7 the author points out that the Melchizedek order is superior to the Levitic on seven counts: the patriarch Abraham gave tithes to Melchizedek (vv. 4-6), Melchizedek the superior blessed Abraham the inferior (v. 7), the Aaronic priesthood was served by mortal men while the Scripture is silent concerning Melchizedek's (v. 8), in the person of Abraham, Levi, still unborn, gave tithes to Melchizedek (vv. 9-10), the Melchizedek order is made permanent in Christ while the Levitic priesthood and the Law were abrogated (vv. 11-19), the Son's appointment by the Father's oath made Melchizedek's order perpetual (vv. 20-22), death caused many vacancies in the Aaronic priesthood while priesthood under the Melchizedek order did not pass to another (vv. 23-24). But in all of this the real cause of the superiority of Christ's Priesthood has not been given. His Priesthood is superior because His Person is superior. His Priesthood is all that He is in Himself. This is evident in two respects.

(i) On His human side. There are four matters here to which we shall refer briefly.

(a) He was made like unto His brethren (2:17). Those whom He would redeem were mortal men, subject to the frailty of the flesh, and in bondage to the fear of death; so Jesus Christ had to take part with them in flesh and blood, and even become obedient unto death. It was through His humiliation and death that He freed them from their bondage (2:3, 10).

(b) He was "touched with the feeling of our infirmities" (4:15). "Infirmities" are those moral and physical weaknesses which in themselves may not be wrong, but which may become occasions of stumbling if temptations are allowed to lay hold of them. With these, and with the circumstances that give rise to temptation, Jesus is able to sympathize, because He has suffered with us (Rom. 8:17, I Cor. 12:26).

(c) He "hath been in all points tempted like as we are" (4:15). "Tempted" means tried or tested. Our High Priest, having been schooled in trial, now sympathizes with His sorely tempted brethren, and bears gently with them (5:2). Jesus Christ's temptations, however, stemmed not from within but from outward circumstances (cf. 2:14, 18; 5:7; 12:2; 13:12) : He remained sinless, being an Overcomer. His experience of trial ensures His sympathy with us; His triumph in trial ensures His intercession for us.

(d) He "learned obedience by the things which he suffered" (5:8). While being schooled in trial Jesus learned obedience, perfect submission, to the Father's will. In order to become Savior and perfect High Priest, the Son had to learn this in the circumstances of His earthly life. This obedience was laid upon Him throughout the entire span of His life, and was an ever-deepening experience of what obedience was, and what it cost.

(ii) On His divine side. There are several important details here, but we have space only to refer to them briefly.

(a) He was called of God (5:10). That is to say, He was designated, not invited, to become High Priest. The Father hailed Him as High Priest when He appeared in the heavenly sanctuary; and styling Him thus He installed Him Priest forever.

(b) He is living "after the power of an endless life" (7:16). The phrase "endless [or indissoluble] life" is important. The Aaronic priests were appointed to the ministry, not because they were fitted for it spiritually but because of parentage. Even if they were unwilling, or unfitted, to enter the priesthood they were obliged to do so. Our High Priest, however, came to His office because of what He was in Himself. His life was such that death could not dissolve it. It had an energy and a power that both compelled and enabled Jesus Christ to be a Priest.

(c) Christ is "a priest for ever" (7:17). He is this in virtue of His indestructible life, of course, but also because His order was that of Melchizedek.

(d) He is at the right hand of God (8:1). When Christ took His place at the throne of the Majesty in the heavens to fulfill His High Priesthood He assumed a pre-eminence that was His by right. He became a royal Priest. His kingly status was wedded to His priestly status. His exaltation as High Priest was proclaimed, as were also the finality of His sacrifice for sins and the efficacy of His intercessions.

(e) He "ever liveth to make intercession" for us (7:25). It is principally in intercession that Christ now acts as our High Priest. Through His intercessions we receive help in the hour of trial, we are enabled to hold fast to the end, and are being saved to the uttermost and made heirs of the promises. Through His intercession Jesus accomplishes His complete salvation by bringing us near to God, ensuring our acceptance with God and the supply of all our needs. But this, and all else, Jesus Christ, as our High Priest, is able to perform because He is, in an absolute sense, the Son of God. He is the "heir of all things, the brightness of the Father's glory, the express image of the Father's person, of whom it is said, Thy throne, O God, is for ever and ever."

6. And now, what of the ministry of this great High Priest? What is it that He does for us now in glory? Many answers could be given to that question. For example, He makes reconciliation for the sins of the people; He becomes the Author of eternal salvation; He becomes our Representative within the veil; He enables us to participate in fellowship with God. The most comprehensive answer, however, is given in Hebrews 5:1. Jesus Christ our High Priest has been ordained for men in things pertaining to God. He ministers on our behalf toward God in atoning sacrifice. Or, more simply still, He represents us to God. This He does in two ways.

(i) The first has relevance to sin and transgression; and there are several matters that should be noticed here.

(a) Once admit the exceeding sinfulness of sin in man, and the awful holiness of God, then certain conditions require to be fulfilled before approach to God becomes possible. It is significant here that in the Epistle to the Hebrews our Lord's High-Priesthood is placed in the closest possible connection with His sacrifice on the cross and with His entrance into the Holy of Holies with the blood of that sacrifice. These two events are held together in Hebrews: the historical event of Calvary (12:12) and Christ's entering into the Holy Place in heaven itself to appear in the presence of God for us (9:12-24). On the Day of Atonement the flesh of the offerings was taken outside the camp and burned with fire; so Christ suffered outside the gate in order to sanctify or purify the people by His blood (cf. Titus 2:14). But in Hebrews this latter event is related to the Lord's entering into the heavenly sanctuary. He entered there with His blood shed at Calvary to be our High Priest (9:12-24). His blood has both an atoning and a cleansing efficacy. The fountain has been opened for sin and uncleanness (Zech. 13:1). Sin has been annulled completely by Jesus Christ (9:27), and He has brought us nigh to God (I Pet. 3:18).

(b) We are not to understand from this, however, that our High Priest is now perpetually offering Himself to God for us. Jesus Christ, we must remember, is now a Victor seated on a throne. His offering of Himself on the cross was not only unique;

it was complete (7:27, 9:12-28). Whereas the Levitical high priest was required to offer sacrifice daily, this necessity is not laid upon the Melchizedek High Priest because His offering of Himself was made once and for all (9:12, 26, 28; 10:10, 14; Rom. 6:10). Just as there was no altar in the Holy of Holies in the earthly sanctuary, so there is no altar in the heavenly sanctuary. Because Jesus Christ is a royal Priest He is not to be thought of as standing before an altar but as seated on a throne. And because He is there, access to the Father has been secured. Calvary assures us of propitiation; the Ascension to God's right hand assures us of access on the basis of that propitiation.

(c) This entering in by Christ to the Father's presence with His blood has meaning, therefore, for our fellowship with God. It is one of Jesus' main functions as High Priest to offer sacrifice and thereby to establish, and represent in His own Person, the fellowship of God with men. This fellowship is embodied in the priest. Through the priest people draw near to God; through the priest they have fellowship with God and become His people. This was the function of the priest in Israel; but whereas the Israelites were left outside the Holiest by their high priest, our High Priest has taken us in with Him to the throne of grace. His entering in and appearing before God's face (9:25) signifies that He has opened up, and continues to maintain, fellowship with God on behalf of men. By the sacrifice of Himself He has delivered us from the guilt of sin, and now enables us to enter God's presence, the sacred privilege from which all other spiritual blessings flow.

(d) But what is it that makes Jesus Christ's mediation before God still necessary? It is sin. Sin is constantly interrupting the fellowship that He established between us and God. Sin, therefore, cannot be ignored. It is the defilement of sin that is the root cause of the deepest moral problems in human thought and experience. But God has appointed a way for its removal. His own Son whom He appointed High Priest makes propitiation for our sins (2:17). Notice, however, that this propitiation made by Christ acts not only upon God, but upon sin. God, whose love remains unchanged throughout, does not require to be reconciled to us, but we to Him. It was He who foreordained the propitiation made by Christ (Rom. 3:25).

Apparently, in order to put away sin, sacrifice was a necessity, and this sacrifice Jesus provided in His blood. He was at once sacrificial Offering and Priest, and only in this dual capacity could He deal effectively with sin which once rendered impossible, and which may even now interrupt, fellowship between God and men. He put away sin by the sacrifice of Himself (9:26); and the phrase "to put away sin" expresses both the purpose and the effect of Jesus' sacrifice. The annulment of sin was His aim, and this purpose He achieved by the sacrifice of Himself. Whatever sacrificial illustration is pressed into service to set forth Christ's offering of Himself in His blood — the sin-offering, the covenant-offering, the offering on the Day of Atonement — the expiatory significance is common to them all. Each represents God's way of dealing with sin as a hindrance to man's communion with God.

It was, moreover, on the basis of grace alone, that God worked. By the grace of God Christ tasted death for every man (2:9). And because it was by grace that Jesus died, His redemptive death was as much the expression of the Father's love as it was of the Son's obedience. It was by the enabling grace of the Father that the Son died for all. The Priesthood of the Redeemer was the Father's appointment and calling. It was the Father's will the Son came to do; and since His death was a response in terms of perfect obedience to the Father's will, the Cross is supremely a revelation of the mind, the will, the love of the Father.

(e) The Scriptures do not make clear, however, precisely what in the nature of God was related to Jesus' death, or what created the necessity in God's nature for Jesus' divinely appointed death. They do make clear that Christ's death was His voluntary response to the Father's holy and gracious will *and* to the sinner's dilemma. If it be asked, Why did the Father's gracious will *and* the sinner's dilemma demand, and why were they satisfied by, Christ's loving response in His death? we can only answer with James Denney that in the New Testament sin and death are so inextricably identified with one another that no one could ever hope to undertake the responsibility of sin without submitting to death. Christ was required to die the death of the cross to become the Savior from sin. Everywhere in the New Testament it is the death of Christ *alone* that annuls sin. And — blessed be the God and Father of our Lord Jesus Christ — this Saviour from sin is now become our High Priest, He now represents us, in our sin and need, to a holy God, and He is now making intercession for us.

(ii) Intercession is the second main function which the exalted Lord now fulfills in His High-Priestly activity in the heavenlies. One wonders with James Denney if we moderns have not lost the key to the conception of our Lord's intercession for us. In his *Studies in Theology* (p. 162), he points out that "the apostles mention this sacred function with a kind of adoring awe," and he suggests that "it seems to have impressed them as one of the unimaginable wonders of redemption." "Christ Jesus that died, yea rather that is risen again, who is at the right hand of God, who also maketh intercession for us" — that great Pauline conviction is echoed in Hebrews in the words, ". . . seeing he ever liveth to make intercession" (7:25). And St. John adds his testimony in his first Epistle: "If any man sin, we have an Advocate with the Father, Jesus Christ the righteous" (2:1).

But how shall we understand Christ's intercession for us? Not necessarily that it is expressed in words; and certainly not that it is a continual offering of Himself to God; nor that Jesus Christ being before the throne is a ceaseless reminder to the Father that He died for us. Rather, Christ represents us before the throne, and in and through Him we come to the Father to worship Him. Perhaps the prayer in John 17 may give us some indication as to how we should understand the Lord's intercession for us. He effects the sinner's entrance to the Father's presence, effects the sinner's acceptance by the Father, and effects the supply of the sinner's needs out of His own divine resources of grace and power. Jesus Christ's intercession covers all the sinner's needs.

In this sublime act of intercession our Lord's High Priesthood finds full expression. That Jesus Christ prays for us is an impressive thought; and it becomes doubly impressive when we recall that He intercedes for us as the Lord of Glory. Not with strong crying and tears does He intercede for us now, but with kingly sovereignty that is divine and all-prevailing. His intercession for us, however, is based upon sympathy and sacrifice; and He has power to sympathize with, and exercise mercy toward, the ignorant and the erring as a faithful and merciful High Priest because He shared our nature, our experiences, our temptations. Jesus Christ knows what human life is. This suggests that a ceaseless appeal to His work of reconciliation accomplished on the cross, and a recalling to His mind of the perpetual needs of men still tried and tempted as He Himself was, are involved in Christ's intercessions.

We must not assume that an absent heavenly High Priest is unable to sympathize with us. He does feel for us (4:15). And it is with "our infirmities" that He sympathizes, the things that make it difficult for us to resist temptation. Jesus feels for us there because here He Himself experienced temptation. Apparently the Savior experienced the difficulty of being righteous during His Incarnation. He understands what it means to be subjected to the pressures that induce us to sin. His divine Sonship may have made His personal victory over sin a foregone conclusion but that does not minimize the reality of His temptations, nor the necessity that was laid upon Him to avail Himself of the same means of grace by which we now may triumph. And because He came through temptation victoriously (12:2), sin apart, so may we by His divine succor (2:18). And how does He succor the tempted? His heavenly aid is found at the throne of grace (4:16), and is mediated by the Spirit of grace (10:29). The Spirit brings to the mind of the tempted the things of Christ (John 16:14) and the immediacy of Jesus' High-Priestly sympathy (4:15; 5:1, 2, 14). Thus He reminds them that they are living in vital fellowship with Christ in the very midst of their temptations.

Our High Priest's intercessions for us mean that we are never forgotten by Him; that He who made Himself one with us in life and death in salvation is still consciously identified with us in His High-Priestly ministry; and that we derive now from the soul of Christ the same great support which, during His incarnational life, was the stay of the disciples as they endeavored to love and serve Him. This is salvation to the uttermost, salvation that is the daily, hourly, moment-by-moment experience of the Christian, as the Greek present tense "to save" in 7:25 suggests. As each emergency arises Jesus Christ keeps on intervening in saving power on the believer's behalf. And He keeps on saving "to the uttermost," wholly or completely. But the Christian has a responsibility in this matter. The Lord saves him moment by moment in the measure in which he keeps on coming to God through Him. The fact that the content, or the object, of our great High Priest's intercessions is not specified may be taken to mean that no matter what the Christian's need may be at any time the intercession by the Son effects the supply of that need. In His High-Priestly intercession for us, Christ, as our Advocate with the Father, interprets our needs, collectively and individually, and pleads our cause prevailingly, doubtless in a manner similar to the intercessory prayer in John 17.

If our Lord's High-Priestly ministry means all this, it must affect our own life in Him, and our witness for Him. Inescapably it will become a powerful motive for a consistent, God-glorifying, Christian life on our part. It will teach us more and more to rest in the love of this unseen but ever-present Friend whose faithfulness neither changes nor decays. It will anchor our souls to the conviction that the undying love and the power of our High Priest are constantly directed toward us, not merely when we pray, but uninterruptedly.

7. We should notice, finally, what it is that our glorified Lord's High-Priestly ministry guarantees for us. His High-Priesthood secures for us three things of great importance.

(i) Jesus Christ's High Priesthood guarantees the priesthood of all believers. There are several matters to notice here.

(a) It is true that Christ's Priesthood is complete. It admits of no rivalry. There is nothing left for a successor to do. The term priesthood, however, is applied in the New Testament to the members of the Christian community, irrespective of office or distinction. For example, the Church is spoken of as a "holy priesthood" (I Pet. 2:5) and "a royal priesthood" (I Pet. 2:9). And in Revelation 1:6, 5:6, 20:6 the phrase "priests unto God" occurs.

Every believer is a priest unto God (Rev. 1:5) but he can draw near to God to fulfill his priestly functions only as he is sprinkled with the blood of Christ, and washed in the water of baptism (Eph. 5:26, Tit. 3:5, I Pet. 3:21, and cf. Ex 30:20). The priesthood to which the believer belongs is a holy priesthood unto God, it is God's "spiritual house" or temple. As a member of it the believer can approach God through Jesus, the new and living way, and serve God before the throne. This holy priesthood is also a royal priesthood. As both royal and priestly functions were united in Christ, so are kingship and priesthood in the believer. In the kingdom of God saints reign with the King of kings, and serve Him as priests. The redeemed are formed into God's kingdom and become priests who are invested with royal power. And the Greek present tense in Revelation 5:10 reminds us that the believers' kingly rank and priestly functions are present realities in spite of persecution and hatred in this world, though Revelation 20:6 emphasizes the future aspect.

(b) The significance of this is that, whereas the high priest under the old dispensation left the people outside when he penetrated the Holy of Holies, Jesus Christ our High Priest carried His people with Him within the veil, and gave them access to the Father when He entered the heavenly sanctuary through the blood of His cross (10:19-22). The boldness or joyful confidence here spoken of in 10:19 (cf. also 3:6, II Cor.

7:4, Acts 2:29, 4:13, Eph. 3:12, where the same word occurs) is founded upon the sufficiency of Jesus' sacrifice for sin. The believer's approach to the throne of grace, however, is not *with* but *by* or *through* the blood of Christ, which effectively inaugurated the way of access to the Father. That which was the prerogative of the priestly caste in the Old Testament now belongs to every Christian; and he can keep on exercising this prerogative with that total engagement which genuine worship requires, and with full assurance that it is the way to favor and fellowship with God. Thus the divine ideal expressed in Exodus 19:6, "Ye shall be unto me a kingdom of priests," was transferred to, and fulfilled in, the Christian Church.

(c) At this point it is necessary to insist that these priestly rights are common to all believers. They are distributed equally among all to whom Christ has given access to the throne of grace. All enjoy the priestly privilege of access to the Father, the God of all grace. All are enjoined to participate in the priestly act of offering sacrifices to God (13:5). In the New Testament it is to a Father that the believer comes, through Christ the Elder Brother. That is to say, in the experience of Christians their sonship and their priesthood are identical. The sonship of believers inescapably involves the priesthood of believers, and vice versa. The priesthood of believers is simply a function of their sonship with God, otherwise it does not have any meaning at all.

(d) We have already noticed that there is no sacrifice for sin in the New Testament except the sacrifice which Christ offered once for all. This sacrifice is the new and living way by which every Christian has the right of approach to the throne. Since this means that the believer's approach is by or through Jesus (13:15), he can dispense with every ancient or modern ritual ordinance or levitical device which claims to assist men in their drawing near to God. In addition, since every believer is a priest, none requires the mediation of any members of a so-called priesthood who, claiming to be nearer God than their fellows, usurp to themselves the office of mediator between God and men. Writing to believers in general, Peter addresses them as a holy priesthood who themselves offer up spiritual sacrifices that are acceptable to God through Jesus Christ (I Pet. 2:5).

The New Testament betrays no knowledge of, or interest in, a distinctly priestly class in the Church whose task it is to mediate between God and men. Christianity is what it is — a perfect and an abiding fellowship with God — because it is realized in the eternal Son of God. It cannot be realized or guaranteed in any other. To introduce into the Church official mediators is to relapse from the Melchizedek to the Aaronic priesthood, and is to introduce an apostasy into New Testament Christianity. There is in the New Testament no trace of any Christian priesthood making sacrifice for sin in order to mediate between God and man. On the other hand, the New Testament is equally sure that the simplest believer has the indefeasible right of access to God through Jesus Christ the great High Priest. No artificial system of mediation dares to prevent him from standing in person before the Father through Christ.

(e) But it is not sufficient only to insist that in the Protestant doctrine of the priesthood of all believers there is an avowal of every Christian's right to approach God through Christ, and an access to the spiritual blessings in Christ Jesus in the heavenlies. It is this attitude that has led to a weakening of this doctrine. One must also understand that priesthood for the believer involves responsibility as well as privilege. It involves sacrifice. We are all called to be priests unto God, but each has his sacrifice to offer, the offering of himself, and of his service, to Jesus Christ in terms of intercession, as well as witness and Christian living. Priesthood makes searching demands upon Christian priests. Inescapably it demands self-sacrifice upon the altar of Christian service, the obligation to carry out in daily life the uttermost implication of belonging to Christ.

(f) But it implies supremely the duty of prayer and intercession in the name of Jesus Christ our Mediator (John 14:12-13, 15:16, 16:23-24). We have already noticed (pp. 30ff.) that one of the conditions that Christ attached to the believer's priestly intercessions was that he intercede in His name. How are we to understand this condition? The use of any name involves a man in union with the person whose name he is using. It may also include the enforcing of the will of the person whose name is used, and the furthering of his interests. So in priestly intercession in the name of Christ: it means to pray in union with the Lord, and to offer prayers whose principal aim will be to extend His kingdom. And as the apostles learned long ago in the upper room, so the believer as priest today learns that one of his dearest joys and privileges is to participate in a continuing experience of the efficacy of Christ's name in prayer. To pray in Jesus' name is to acknowledge that in and through Him all prayer and communion with the Father takes place. Through

Christ even thanks are offered to the Father (Rom. 1:8). To pray in the name of Christ means to pray as the representative of Christ, and to pray in the same spirit as Christ Himself prayed. Even the answer to prayer is in Christ's name (John 16:23).

(g) One may well ask, Who is sufficient for these things? The answer is that in fulfilling our priestly task at this high level we can count upon the help of an Advocate, other than our great High Priest, namely, the Holy Spirit. While our High Priest intercedes for us in glory, the Holy Spirit intercedes for us in the depths of our own hearts (Rom. 8:26-27). The truth of the matter is that this priestly ministry is so sacred, and so demanding, that it involves the working of the Holy Spirit with man on earth, and the working of the Son for man in the heavenlies. The Holy Spirit inspires the prayer or intercession in the heart of the priestly believer on earth; the High Priest in glory presents it to the Father, and in His name claims its acceptance and fulfillment by the Father.

(ii) Jesus Christ's High Priesthood guarantees the immortality of all believers. Because our exalted Lord has become the Forerunner within the veil, our faith is like an anchor cast into the world beyond. It holds us in secure attachment to that world. In virtue of Jesus Christ's Lordship over all, both in the world to come and in this present world, the believer is called to this world above, and is already tasting its powers (6:5, 2:4). In fellowship with all other members of the Son's household, the believer is a partaker now of a heavenly calling. It is a heavenly calling, not only because it comes from heaven, and is therefore an upward calling unto holiness, but also because Christian is even now in possession of that world that is yet to come. The Lord Jesus Christ who belonged to it, and descended from it at the Incarnation, has revealed it to men; and by returning to it through death, resurrection, and ascension, He has opened it up for us, because it was as our Forerunner (6:20), as well as our High Priest (10:19), that He returned to it.

We must therefore hold fast the confession of our hope of immortality without wavering. It is essential to look back constantly to the past saving deed of Christ on the cross; and it is equally necessary to keep Jesus Christ's present saving activity in His High Priesthood in view; but it is also imperative that we look upward and forward to that world of present eternal reality whither our High Priest has gone to represent us to God and free us from the fear of death. By penetrating the veil behind which lies the world of eternal spiritual reality, Jesus Christ has prepared the way by which we one day are destined to follow Him.

And because He is already there, we too are already come. The Epistle to the Hebrews insists that in a sense we are already there. We have already begun to live in the world to come. The eternal world of reality has already projected itself into this transitory world of unreality. The world to come has already broken into the closing epoch of this present age. This truth is illustrated in Abraham who by faith already possessed Canaan, even though he spent his life in tents, now here, now there (11:10). Our present access to God through Jesus Christ is a genuine anticipation of future bliss (12:22-24). His High-Priestly service has even now inaugurated the coming era, and permits us even now to taste "the heavenly gift . . . and the powers of the world to come." Already we have come to Mount Zion, the city of the living God, the heavenly Jerusalem, to myriads of angels in festal gathering, to the assembly of the firstborn enrolled in heaven (3:1, 12:22-23).

Jerusalem on earth was the dwelling place of God in symbol (Ps. 76:2, 146:10, 9:11), but the heavenly Jerusalem (cf. Gal. 4:26, Rev. 21:2) is His dwelling place in truth. Into it all His people will be gathered, and there He will manifest Himself to them in the fullness of His glory. With myriads of angelic beings the members of the Church of the Firstborn have their rights and destinies in this new Jerusalem; and a joyous company they will be at the last, as the Greek for "general assembly" (lit. "festal assembly") suggests. And it is to God Himself they will come.

We must again remind ourselves, however, that Christians have already come into this fellowship of eternal realities. Living in the earth, their citizenship is in heaven (Luke 10:20; Rom. 8:16; 29; Phil. 3:20, RV; James 1:18), and this glorious communion of the saints above and on earth Jesus Christ the one and only Mediator has effected through His blood which speaks better things than the blood of Abel. Abel's blood cried, "Vengeance!" Jesus' blood cries, "Salvation." Paul also adds his testimony to our having been delivered from this present evil age (Gal. 1:4). The truth of the matter seems to be that we are now as children of God living a double life! *Actually* we are still living within the lower earthly order, *ideally* we have already transcended it, and are now confidently anticipating the moment when the actual and the ideal shall be identical. But even now, by faith, the ideal is translated into the real. If we have been delivered from this present evil age in very truth through faith in Christ, then we can maintain, "We have been reconciled through the death of his Son; much more shall we be saved by his life." It is from Christ's present Priestly life that the whole life of grace in the believer springs, an ideal and actual life of victory and power.

(iii) That is why we can say, in the third place, that Jesus Christ's Priesthood guarantees continuance in grace, and growth in grace, for all believers. The author of Hebrews is constantly urging his readers to press on to full growth. At the moment they are babes whose food is milk, and who are without experience (5:13), but they must learn to eat solid food, exercise the senses, and develop spiritual discernment (5:14). The perfection spoken of here and in 6:1 is not sinless perfection but perfection in the sense of maturity, maturity in Christian knowledge, in ability to discern or discriminate between what is superior and what is inferior in matters of instruction, and maturity in faith and doctrine. Only the spiritual man, the Christian who is constantly pressing on to full growth, can so discriminate (I Cor. 2:14f., Rom. 2:18, Phil. 1:9f.). But the writer of Hebrews does more than lay these matters on the conscience of the believers to whom he is writing. He tells them how it is possible that they can press on to full growth. He insists that it is through the High-Priestly ministry of the Lord of Glory that spiritual infancy is left behind, and spiritual maturity is realized; the Law, with its sacrificial system, can never produce spiritual maturity (10:1). Chapter 5, which sets forth the authority and the honor of Jesus Christ's Priesthood, is immediately followed by the command to go on to perfection (6:1). The four following statements are an expansion of this important truth taught in the Epistle to the Hebrews.

(a) It is because we have a High Priest in glory that we can "hold fast our confession" (4:14). The Hebrew Christians were wavering in their confession because they failed to apprehend, or were in danger of forgetting, the truth of the Savior's High Priesthood. Both the incentive, and the enabling dynamic, to hold fast our confession is the apprehension of the truth that He who has passed through the heavens to become our great High Priest is "Jesus," who in His humanity humbled Himself

(2:9) to become one with us, that He might understand us, and "the Son of God," the Messianic King (1:2, 3:6), who in His ascension was exalted to be Lord of all. Hence the necessity to "consider the Apostle and High Priest of our confession, even Jesus" (3:1). Our confession that Jesus is the Christ, the Son of the living God (II Cor. 9:13, I Tim. 6:12), is to be held without wavering (10:23), in the face of the jeers and allurements of an antagonistic world. To this incentive is added the inspiration that derives from the faithfulness of God to His promises. The promises of God are a sure foundation (6:12). They cannot fail because God cannot fail (6:18).

(b) It is because we have a High Priest in glory who has suffered with us and can now sympathize with us, that we can hold fast our confession (4:15f). The writer is sometimes occupied with the aim of our approach to God, that of worship and service (7:25; 10:1, 22; 11:6; 12:18-22), but his main preoccupation is how the approach has become possible. It is because we draw near through our High Priest. True, we come to a throne of grace, but it is a *throne,* and it is the throne of God. Notice the same connection in the Old Testament, symbolized in the mercy-seat above the Ark of the Covenant (Ex. 25:21; cf. Ps. 97:2 with Isa. 16:5). And as we come to the throne through our one and only Mediator, Jesus the Son of God, the throne becomes the source from which mercy and grace are dispensed to the believer.

(c) It is because we have a High Priest in glory that we can draw near to exhort one another to love and good works (10:19-24). The wonder of the boldness here spoken of lies in the fact that it concerns entrance into the Holiest, to the place of God's very throne. The way of boldness of entry thither is the veil of Christ's flesh (cf. 6:19, 9:3). In His Incarnation His flesh barred His entrance to the Father, as the veil in the earthly tabernacle barred the high priest's entrance to the Holiest; and yet the only way into the Holiest was through the veil (this was rent at the Crucifixion, Matt. 27:51) ; so Jesus Christ entered the sanctuary above through the rent veil of His flesh. And this is the way by which we draw near to the throne. But we must walk this way with uprightness of heart, fullness of faith, removal of the consciousness of guilt through Christ's sacrifice and the washing of the body with pure water (probably the water of baptism) ; and we each draw near by this new and living way to find grace, and to worship and serve God (4:16, 7:25, 10:22, 11:6). We must also draw near in company with our fellow believers, for worship and mutual edification (cf. Acts 2:42), and to stimulate each to love and serve the other in good works (6:10, 13:16).

(d) It is because we have a High Priest in glory through whom we have received a kingdom that we can draw near to serve God (12:28). In this verse service probably means more than worship. It is the service that we offer God in the world that is marked for destruction (1:11); but because we are kings and priests unto God, and citizens of a kingdom that cannot be shaken, we can "have grace," the grace of divine assistance by which we "serve God" (9:14), with reverence and fear. This is service that involves our going forth outside the camp to bear Christ's reproach (13:12-13). The flesh of the sin-offering was not eaten by the priests (cf. Lev. 4:12, 21), but taken outside the camp and burned with fire. This ordinance found fulfillment in Christ's "suffering without the gate" (Matt. 27:32, John 19:17f), which symbolized the Lord's rejection by the Jews. Christians now must enter into this reproach, and share in the fellowship of His sufferings (cf. 12:2, 11:26). But this Christians are inspired to do because through their High Priest now in glory they receive "grace upon grace."

The service referred to in 12:28 has, however, another interpretation. The most important service we can render to God in virtue of our Lord's High-Priestly ministry in glory is the service we offer before the throne when we draw near through Christ. What is the nature of this service? It may be argued that since all priesthood and sacrifice have been gathered up into the Priesthood and Sacrifice of Jesus Christ there remains now no such ministry for the Christian to fulfill. But this is not so. When the Christian enters the Holiest through the blood of Christ he has a service to fulfill there, a service which is the offering of sacrifice. It is true that the doctrine of the priesthood of all believers is not prominent in the Epistle to the Hebrews, but that is because the writer's over-riding preoccupation is with the Priesthood of the believer's Savior; the Christian nevertheless has a service of sacrifice to perform at the throne. What this service is 13:15-16 makes clear.

It is first "the sacrifice of praise." This sacrifice may be offered "continually," because it is a spiritual sacrifice, and because the believer has access to the throne at all times (10:19). The subject of this sacrifice of praise is God's gifts, especially His unspeakable Gift. But "to do good" (13:16) is also included in "such sacrifices," with which "God is well pleased." A believer's deeds of mercy in ministering to the needs of the afflicted are a sacrifice unto God. But whatever the sacrifice may be that we offer as priests at the throne, it can be offered to God only "through" (13:15) Jesus Christ the great High Priest in glory.

If we want to be growing, fruitful Christians, full of confidence and faith, then we must seize hold of all the wonderful privileges that Christ our High Priest has placed within our reach through His entering in through the veil. Let us draw near to God through Christ, and let us keep near to God through Christ; then we shall go on to perfection. A maturing Christian experience, a joyous Christian testimony, an abounding Christian service are possible only as we draw near to the throne of grace boldly, often, and in full assurance of faith, through our great High Priest, to appropriate to the full the blessings that Christ's High Priesthood in glory mediates to us.

CHAPTER SIX

WAIT ON THE LORD

WE HAVE REACHED a critical point in our study of the Lord's doctrine and practice of prayer. The time has come when we must again raise the question, What does all this mean for us? The question was asked earlier in our study (pp. 53ff.), What significance has Christ's prayer life for us today? but it must be faced again in a much fuller way, now that Christ's life of prayer has been seen more fully.

We may begin our answer by turning to Luke 11:1, and noting how the disciples responded to our Lord's life of prayer. Coming upon Jesus "praying in a certain place," they asked Him to teach them how to pray. In effect they were saying, "Lord, we do not know how to pray, but we want to learn; so please teach us to pray." In this confession and request there are four important matters which are meaningful for our practice of prayer.

1. The disciples' confession was made spontaneously. Our Lord's heart must have leaped for joy when the Twelve made this request of Him. Since prayer meant so much for Him, He must often have grieved over their lack of interest in prayer, their lack of desire to engage in prayer. He must often have yearned to have them make this request of Him; but doubtless He had decided not to hurry them on prematurely toward this goal. The request must come spontaneously, and out of a sense of personal need. To elicit this request before they were ready to understand the full significance of it, or were ready to receive Christ's answer to it, would simply have demonstrated both the danger and the futility of premature growth in spiritual experience. And so the Lord decided to bide His time until the Twelve, by a spontaneous request, showed they were ready to take this all-important forward step in their understanding and experience of prayer. The signal of their readiness was this entirely voluntary and spontaneous request that the Lord should teach them to pray.

2. The request was made by men who were not entirely ignorant of prayer. Many today would describe them as praying men. Indeed, not only was there a sense in which the Twelve

understood what prayer was; they were in the habit of engaging regularly in prayer.

This candid request was, from our standpoint, completely unexpected when it is remembered that the disciples were all pious and faithful worshippers in their local synagogues. They knew, and would themselves use, the set forms of prayer followed in the Jewish church. Doubtless they had often led the public prayers in their local synagogues, since this was the prerogative of every male Jew once he became a *bar mitsvah*. And doubtless, too, these great synagogal prayers were meaningful and dear to them, in the measure in which they were patriotic and practicing Jews. In that sense they were praying men. But in spite of their deep love for, and habitual participation in, the beautiful forms of prayer used in the synagogue services, they had come to realize that they did not really know how to pray. Here was an area of the religious life to which they, deeply religious men though they might be, were almost total strangers. After years of religious life and piety, they were only now beginning to distinguish between saying prayers and praying.

3. The request from the Twelve was, in fact, a most unusual admission of ignorance; and often such a humble, and humbling, confession is the first step to blessing and progress in the spiritual life. In many respects it was an unusual and unexpected confession; and yet it was not so shattering an acknowledgment as that made by Paul in Romans 8:26 where we read, "We know not how to pray as we ought." We have ample evidence in his Epistles that Paul was a man of prayer in the profoundest sense of that much used phrase. Some of his experiences had been so intense that on occasion he felt that he had been lifted completely outside of himself (cf. II Cor. 12:1ff.). Many a time, as is plain from some examples of his prayers in the Ephesian Epistle, Paul's spirit soared high in his desire for communion with God. And yet in Romans 8:26 he confesses, "We know not that which we should pray for according as it behooves."

In this deeply spiritual sense, the disciples' admission of ignorance concerning prayer in Luke 11:1 is not to be compared with the Apostle's in Romans 8:26, and yet, because it marked a completely new point of departure in their religious experience, it was profoundly significant. Not that they would now immediately disparage the great synagogal prayers as being an outmoded medium of worship, or treat with contempt those who used them. On the contrary, this new insight into the meaning of prayer to which Jesus Christ was admitting them would make the set forms of public prayer more meaningful to them. It would enable them to enter into the import of their language. They would seize the spirit and purpose of the synagogal prayers in a new way, until these great utterances of the worshipping heart would become a means of grace to them in a way hitherto unknown.

4. This was the more certain, not only because they acknowledged they did not really know what it was to pray, but also because they were willing to learn: hence their earnest and spontaneous request, "Lord, teach us to pray." They would not understand all that their request implied or involved. Indeed, our Lord might well have answered this request in the same way in which He answered the request made by James and John through their mother: "Ye know not what ye ask" (Matt. 19:21f.). But the Twelve were desirous of learning how to pray. They were willing to enroll in Christ's school of prayer. They did not then realize that this was a school from which one never graduates, a school in which one always remains a learner, kneeling with the Teacher; but they were at least willing to begin to learn.

"Lord, teach us to pray." That in summary was the disciples' response to our Lord's life of prayer. And the preceding chapters have been written in the hope that our Lord's teaching and practice of prayer will invoke, in the minds of readers, the same response that it did in the minds of the Twelve. We again turn, therefore, to that divine life of prayer, to learn how to pray as we ought. In endeavoring to achieve this aim, use will be made of the great Old Testament phrase, "Wait on the Lord."

It is altogether appropriate that some Old Testament material should be included in a book whose subject is Christ's teaching and practice of prayer. The Lord's own prayer life must have been rooted in, and nourished by, this rich fertile soil. From His earliest years Jesus Christ would be an eager student of the Old Testament. Inevitably the ancient Scriptures would be worked into His personality. He would be truly a Man of the Book. Indeed, it is of the highest probability that the Old Testament's use of this very phrase, "Wait on the Lord," was one of the basic inspirational influences in our Lord's prayer life. Who knows but the facts of His devotional life which have been examined in the preceding chapters may very well reflect the effect, the ascendancy, and the moral power that it exercised over His mind and spirit.

Certain it is that the Old Testament would be entirely indispensable in Jesus Christ's life of devotion and communion with the Father.   Just as the Bible is indispensable to us for the development and nourishment of our devotional life, so the Old Testament was for the Lord a necessary means of fellowship with the Father.   That is why sayings from the Old Testament, long pondered and prayed over in the solitude of the hills of Nazareth, would in later years leap spontaneously to his mind, and become an integral part of the triumphs that He won in the critical moments of His earthly ministry: for example, in the moving moment of His vocation in baptism, in the temptation period, and consistently throughout the entire ministry, and even in death.

All these crises reflect the attitude and poise of spirit in One whose mind was steeped in the Old Testament, One who had long since reached to the heart of the meaning of, and who had come habitually to act upon, the Old Testament injunction that is now before us, "Wait on the Lord."   This being so, the probability is that a study of this Old Testament phrase will serve a dual purpose: to map the path of obedience for those who wish to respond to the challenge of our Lord's teaching and practice of prayer, and to supplement the primary topic that has been before us at various points.

At the outset of an inquiry into the Old Testament use of this great injunction, "Wait on the Lord," one is immediately confronted by a difficulty.   The difficulty stems from the great familiarity with which the phrase is used today.   In this instance, however, familiarity does not breed contempt; it breeds confusion. We are so conversant with the phrase that we assume that we know what it means, whereas, as is the case with so many hackneyed terms and familiar institutions, we are really quite hazy about the actual significance.   The phrase, "Wait on the Lord," comes to us surrounded by an aura of sanctity from the past.   Custom has so robbed it of its original content that it is often used inconsiderately by us today.   It is still a pious phrase, but the sharp outline of its real meaning has been blurred.   For the majority of us the phrase is a general term which describes the prayer life.   To wait on the Lord is to pray to the Lord.   When the Hebrew original is examined, however, (it seems to have no real counterpart in the New Testament), the phrase is found to bear the stamp of real individuality.   It has a quite specific meaning, and is not just part of the jargon of religious life.

It should be noted that the words "Wait on the Lord" (they

occur in the Old Testament several times with certain variations),
do not always imply waiting upon God *in prayer*. The phrase
sometimes seems to mean to be patient, to wait until God inter-
venes on one's behalf. For example, one cannot be certain that
when the prophet announced, "They that wait for Jehovah shall
renew their strength" (Isa. 40:31), that he was thinking specifically in terms of prayer. But there is good ground for understanding the phrase to mean in several instances, Wait on the
Lord in prayer.

It cannot be without significance that the phrase is found most
frequently in the Psalms. The Psalms are pre-eminently the
literature of the waiting heart, and in this devotional literature
our phrase occurs, with variations, at least fifteen times. The
phrase also appears in similar literature of the worshipping
heart in the Old Testament. The book of Isaiah repeats it seven
times. In the prophecies of Hosea, Micah, and Jeremiah, it occurs
once in each instance. The phrase is also found once in Proverbs.
This distribution suggests that the phrase "Wait on the Lord"
was often on the lips of men who were pre-eminently men of
prayer. To them it described the chief exercise of the human
spirit in the devotional life. Obviously, then, although the Old
Testament phrase, "Wait on the Lord," is not, in the strictest
sense, always synonymous with prayer to God, yet it is so patently
a part of the language of the praying heart, and it so perfectly
expresses the primary attitude of the man of devout life toward
God, that it has come to be understood in terms of waiting
upon God *in prayer*.

When one examines the Hebrew original, one finds that the
Authorized Version of the Scriptures has not done justice to the
original language by its repeated use of the word "wait" to
translate the different Hebrew words which carry this idea. The
Hebrew uses no fewer than eight different words for the idea of
waiting upon God. An examination of those Hebrew words will
show that they contain much that is deeply significant for the
Christian today.

As we examine these eight Hebrew words, it is important for
us constantly to recall that they occur in those areas of the Old
Testament that were particularly favored by our Lord when He
was on earth and that were used by Him as the sword of the
Spirit in the great crises of His life and work. There is what
has been called, "an inner canon of Scripture" for our Lord in

the Hebrew Bible.* This inner canon seems to have included two of the Old Testament books in which the urgency for waiting upon the Lord comes most frequently to expression, namely, the Psalms and Isaiah. It also included Hosea, where the phrase occurs once. This inevitably means that Jesus must often have had this Old Testament ideal before Him as He read the ancient Jewish Scriptures and as He prayed. Indeed, it would become a powerfully formative influence in His own prayer life as He grew up from boyhood, through adolescence, to manhood. In fact, the phrase may be taken as the quintessential expression of His prayer life. For Him prayer was, in essence, waiting upon the Lord. That this was so is evident from another fact that emerges. It will be found that the eight Hebrew words rendered invariably by "Wait on the Lord" in the AV, correspond fairly closely to the eight key words which set forth our Lord's teaching on the nature of prayer (see Chapter I).

1. The first group of words which we shall consider expresses the demand for *humility*, which we found to be implicit in our Lord's teaching on the nature of prayer (p. 15). The words come from the Hebrew roots *dūm* or *dāmam*, and are found in Psalm 62:65 and Lamentations 3:26. The Authorized Version translates the words in question by "wait," but the Hebrew words really mean to be silent, still, or quiet.

The true meaning of the two Hebrew roots is clear from their use, for example, in Leviticus 10:3, where, after Nadab and Abihu had offered strange fire before the Lord, Aaron their father holds his peace, probably in shame and distress. Again, in Exodus 15:16, the Canaanites are said to be still as a stone, that is to say, struck dumb with astonishment and dread. Silence caused by profound grief and dismay is referred to in Lamentations 2:10, 3:28, while in Psalm 107:29 God settles the storm into a whisper. It was altogether appropriate that this thought of silence should be related in Scripture to the soul's waiting upon God in prayer because, essentially, to wait before God is to be still before God. In Psalm 62 the AV reads, "Truly my soul waiteth upon God" (v. 1); and again, "My soul, wait thou only upon God" (v. 5). But the Hebrew of verse 1 actually has the noun for silence or repose, where the AV has "waitheth"; while verse 5 has the imperative, be silent, which the AV has rendered "wait." In this

*See my article "Christ and the Old Testament" in the *Expository Times*, Vol. lxvii, No. 1, Oct. 1955, where this is worked out in greater detail.

connection it is interesting to notice that a literal translation of Psalm 65:1 would be, "To thee silence is praise, O God, in Zion."

A similar emphasis on silence in our waiting upon the Lord is present in Lamentations 3:26: "It is good that a man should both hope and quietly wait for the salvation of the Lord." Perhaps a better reading would be, "It is good that one should hope quietly for the salvation of the Lord." That this verse should be understood in terms of waiting before God in prayer is clear from the preceding verse, where it is asserted that the Lord is good to those who seek Him. The same connection between stillness and prayer is even more strongly emphasized in Psalm 37:7, where the poet urges his readers, "Be silent unto the Lord and wait longingly for him." In the Septuagint version of Psalm 61:5 and 37:7 the Greek translators understood the silence of worshipful waiting upon God in the sense of submission or resignation which further enriches this whole concept of quietness and repose in our prayer life. And since this involves humility, it answers to an essential element in Jesus' teaching on prayer.

Now this stillness of heart is an important and essential factor in our own waiting before the Lord in prayer. The loss of the secret of stillness and silence in worship and adoration impoverishes devotional life and renders ineffective much of our waiting upon God in prayer. It is essential to recollect our thoughts and quiet our hearts at the commencement of prayer (see pp. 84ff.). "Jehovah is in his holy temple; let all the earth keep silence before him" (Hab. 2:20) is a word that should be in our thoughts as we enter the secret place; or as the psalmist expressed it, "Be silent unto the Lord, and wait longingly for him" (Ps. 37:7). It is during this period of stillness that we search our hearts and know our thoughts and take heed to our ways and humble ourselves as the Publican did in the Lord's parable. It is then, too, that we remember the Lord God, and recall His grace and power; and thus prepare ourselves for that highest of all activities in which the human spirit can participate — communion with God.

2. The next Hebrew word we shall consider answers to the element of *intensity*, which, as our Lord underlined in His teaching, is of the essence of prayer (see p. 19). The root is *qāwāh*, and is full of interest and significance for the Christian. The Oxford Hebrew and English Lexicon suggests that originally *qāwāh* meant to twist or to stretch. Later it came to mean tension, to be on the stretch. In Arabic it means a strand of rope, or a many-stranded and, therefore, a strong rope. In Syriac the root

is used of thread. It is easy to see how a word that conveys the idea of tension should be used of enduring, or waiting with patient endurance. These two meanings may be said to be united in the noun that has been formed from this Hebrew root: the noun is *tiqwāh*, which means (a) a rope or cord (Josh. 2:18, 21); and (b) hope (Ruth 1:12), the ground of hope (Job 4:6, Ps. 71:5), or the thing hoped for (Ezek. 19:5, Job 6:8, Prov. 24:14).

The root *qāwāh* is frequently used in the Old Testament in its ordinary sense of waiting, although the idea of strain or tension is often added to the thought of waiting. For example, it occurs in Psalm 56:6, where men lie in wait for the psalmist (see also Ps. 119:95). In Isaiah 51:5 it describes the waiting of the coastlands for the Lord's intervention, while in 59:9 it is used of the expectant waiting of men for light, but instead obscurity comes. Now it is this word, which conveys the idea of tension and patient endurance, that is used in the Old Testament of a man's waiting before God in prayer. Clearly, this specific use in the Hebrew Scriptures is significant for us today.

In Psalm 25:3 the assurance is that none that wait upon the Lord shall be ashamed, and what the psalmist means by waiting is plain from verse 1, where he lifts up his soul unto the Lord in prayer. The measure of the intensity here involved is found in the psalmist's use of *qāwāh* in verse 3. The meaning of the word is again filled out in Psalm 69:6, where to wait upon the Lord is paralleled with seeking the Lord. As the psalmist waited before God in the state of tension which *qāwāh* expresses, his spirit sought the Lord with deep yearning. The same connection is established in Lamentations 3:25. The element of intensity in prayer finds expression also in the psalmist's affirmation that the Lord is for him the God of salvation, and he therefore waits for God to guide and teach him (Ps. 25:5).

This tension is also expressed in Psalm 27:14, where the psalmist has to strengthen his resolve to be strong, and to compel his heart to take courage, and to persist in his demanding spiritual exercise which prayer before God involves. The use of a well-known Hebrew idiom in Psalm 40:1 again brings to expression the strong meaning of this word when used with reference to waiting upon God in prayer. The AV of the Hebrew "I waited patiently," points the way here. The idiom was the grammatical device used in Hebrew to strengthen the action of the verb and to add to it the element of certainty. A literal rendering of Psalm 40:1 would be, "Waiting I waited for the Lord."

That this had reference to waiting in prayer before God is clear from the words which complete the first line of this Hebrew poem. Waiting, the psalmist waited for the Lord, and as the strength of purpose and perseverance and desire expressed itself in a pent-up cry, the cry for help of a person in dire trouble, the Lord inclined to the psalmist and effected the deliverance which is so powerfully described in verse 2. This same thought of deliverance is in Psalm 52:9, where the psalmist waits on the name of the Lord, on the Lord, who through His name has made known Himself, His nature, character and purpose. And this waiting on the name of the Lord is done "in the presence of thy saints" (v. 9); that is to say, in the presence of brother Is-raelites who worship as they wait upon the Lord in the fellow-ship of prayer and supplication. Deliverance for those who thus wait is also expressed in Isaiah 25:9, 33:2, Proverbs 20:22. Small wonder, then, that men of prayer, such as Jeremiah (14:22) and Hosea (12:6), should urge their generations to wait only upon God because He only could deliver.

Isaiah 26:8-9 also communicates to us something of what the Hebrews meant when they included this word *qāwāh* in their vocabulary of faith and prayer. That it expressed for them the intensity of the praying man, an intensity manifesting itself in expectation and desire, is clear from the repeated reference to desire in these verses. God's name and memorial is the desire of the waiting people (v. 8). The Lord is desired in the night (in that period when normally the personality is relaxed in the repose of slumber); and even after the tension of spirit in the night watches, the Lord will be sought early (v. 9). The root from which the verb "to seek early" comes means the dawn. This was perhaps the Hebrew way of expressing the diligence and the determination with which it was purposed to seek the Lord. The psalmist's having waited upon God in the night watches would not hinder him from rising early the following morning to continue to wait before the Lord in prayer.

The same figure of speech is used in an even more striking fashion in Psalm 130:5-6. The opening verses clearly point to a waiting in the place of prayer. The degree of intensity that possessed the spirit of this man of prayer is expressed in the con-trast between his waiting and the eager longing of the watchman for the first signs of the dawn, after the slow, silent hours of the night which would often appear interminable to the watchman. In the light of the foregoing the great promise in Isaiah 40:31

becomes much more meaningful because, when the prophet described "they that wait upon the Lord," he used this word *qāwāh* now being considered. It is in the experience of those who wait before the Lord in the manner implied by this word that the great promises are fulfilled: they exchange their strength for the strength of God, they mount up with wings as eagles, they run without wearying, they walk without fainting.

Thus the use of *qāwāh* by Old Testament writers must have been their way of expressing the conviction that waiting upon God in prayer should be characterized by intensity. The man of prayer who thus waits will be on the stretch for God.

Does this Old Testament teaching not throw light on the most intimate insight that the Gospels give us into our Lord's waiting upon the Father in prayer? It may enable us to understand better the grey, drawn face of the Son of God in Gethsemane, and the blood-tinged sweat that stained it. In his account of Christ's Gethsemane experience, Luke tells us quite specifically that it was when He was "in an agony" (*agōnia*), that the Savior "prayed more earnestly" (22:44). (And that such earnest prayer may be a human experience is clear from Colossians 4:12, where Epaphras is described as "always striving" [*agōnizomai*] for the Colossian Church "in prayers.") Now the phrase "more earnestly" in the AV rendering of Luke 22:44 is *ektenesteron*, which comes from a Greek word meaning to stretch or strain. This word conveys exactly the same meaning as the Hebrew *qāwāh*.

Luke uses the same language when describing the prayer life of the Church in Acts 12:5. When Herod had Peter arrested, the Church got to prayer immediately. "Fervent [*ektenēs*] prayer was made of the church unto God" for the imprisoned apostle, whom Herod "was about to bring forth" (v. 6), doubtless for execution. But the Church on her knees (cf. Luke 22:41), and on the stretch, as she waited before God in prayer, proved that that kind of prayer was more potent than Herod Agrippa himself, and more powerful than Herod's prison guard, prison chains, and prison doors. Similar instances of divine intervention would be more common in the Church's experience today were she baptized into some such spiritual agony and intensity, and were she to make it real in her prayer life generally, and in her, intercessions particularly. This would certainly be involved in her obedience to the Lord's teaching and practice of prayer.

3. The next Hebrew word we shall consider expresses yet an-

other feature of our Lord's teaching in prayer: the element of *importunity* (see pp. 12f.). This third root is also very common in the Old Testament, but is used only once in the sense of waiting upon God in prayer. It is the word *chil* or *chül*. Its basic meaning is to twist or writhe. The sense of twisting or writhing is applied to mental anguish (Deut. 2:25, Ps. 55:5), physical pain (Jer. 4:19), the pain of childbirth (Isa. 26:17), and the movement of the body in the dance (Judg. 21:21).

The fact that this powerful metaphor is applied generally to the act of waiting in the Old Testament means that the waiting is not the relaxed waiting characterized by repose, but the tense waiting marked by anguish, suspense, anxiety, mental torture. This is well expressed by Micah: "For the inhabitant of Maroth waiteth anxiously for good, because evil is come down from Jehovah unto the gates of Jerusalem" (1:12). The waiting spoken of here is of someone who is in travail. The metaphor is made more pungent by the fact that in Hebrew the word for inhabitant is feminine, literally, inhabitress. The inhabitress is waiting in the grip of suspense and anxiety as a woman in travail might wait. Waiting in agonized uncertainty is also expressed by use of the same metaphor in Judges 3:25, where the servants of Eglon, king of Moab, not being able to bear the fearful suspense any longer, rush into the room where their royal master is, only to find that he has been murdered.

It is from this root, then, that the word comes in Psalm 37:7, where it is used with reference to waiting upon the Lord in prayer. Interestingly enough, this root, which conveys the idea of suspense and anxiety and mental anguish, is set over against another verb which we have already noticed, a verb which means "to be silent" but which is, in the AV of Psalm 37:7, rendered "rest in the Lord." Hence there is united in this single line of Hebrew poetry both the rest of faith, which reposes silently in God, and the restlessness of faith, which in its silent waiting refuses to be daunted. It waits silently but longingly, and refuses to take "no" for an answer. This dual aspect of faith that waits upon God in prayer, the faith that rests and wrestles, that reposes in silence and writhes in an agony of desire, is well expressed in the Greek translation of Psalm 37:7. The Hebrew, "Be silent unto the Lord," or be still before the Lord, is rendered, "Submit thyself to the Lord." The Greek word used here occurs in II Corinthians 9:13, where Paul refers to the Corinthians having submitted or subjected themselves unto the gospel of Christ; and again in Galatians 2:5, where the apostle affirms

that not for an instant did he submit to the Judaizers. See also
I Timothy 2:11, 3:4, where the same word is used with reference
to the submission of women and of the children of an overseer
in the Church. So the man who is silent unto God as he waits
upon Him is one whose faith is submissive. But this is not the
waiting of passive indifference, as the Greek translators of Psalm
37:7 make clear by rendering the strong verb "to writhe or twist"
in terms of supplication: "Submit thyself unto the Lord, and
supplicate him."

In classical Greek the word in Psalm 37:7 was used in connection with the carrying of an olive branch by a suppliant, the olive
branch symbolizing the fact that he was making supplication.
In Hebrews 5:7 it is used in connection with our Lord's prayer
life in the days of His Incarnation: "In the days of his flesh . . .
[he] offered up prayers and *entreaties,*" or supplications. And
the fact that Jesus Christ offered up these entreaties "with strong
crying and tears" is a powerful reminder of Psalm 37:7 where
waiting upon the Lord in prayer is understood in terms of
writhing and twisting in an agony of desire, which the Greek
translators rendered by means of a word which occurs here in
Hebrews 5:7, a verse which points so clearly to the element of
spiritual longing, and anguish, and pure desire, in our Lord's
life of prayer. So overpowering was this spiritual anguish, that
it expressed itself in "strong crying and tears." Those who are
pupils in Christ's school of prayer, and who use as their textbook
the Lord's teaching and practice of prayer, must also labor to
bring into their waiting upon the Lord in prayer the same rest of
faith and wrestling of faith, the silence and the strength of faith,
the submission and the supplication of faith. As both were
wedded in Christ, so both must be united in us as we, in our
waiting upon the Lord in prayer, are silent unto the Lord in an
agony of expectancy that waits until God responds.

4. The next word used in the Old Testament in connection
with waiting upon the Lord in prayer corresponds to yet another
point in Christ's teaching on prayer: *simplicity* is of the essence
of prayer (pp. 17ff.). It is the Hebrew root *chākāh,* and occurs
a number of times. Unlike the three Hebrew words already
considered, the fourth has no significance beyond that of waiting
or tarrying. For example, in II Kings 9:3, Elisha commands one
of the sons of the prophets not to tarry once he has anointed
Jehu to kingship. The four lepers in II Kings 7, after they
found the Syrians had abandoned camp, decided they must not

wait till dawn before telling this news in Samaria (v. 9). There
are many other references to this simple meaning of waiting or
lingering in the Old Testament.

Our immediate concern, however, is with the references in
which *chākāh* is used in connection with the waiting or tarrying
before the Lord in prayer. The use by Hosea of this word is of
special interest. In 6:9, the tang of the word is brought out well
by the prophet where he uses it to describe a band of marauders
waiting in ambush for an unsuspecting victim. This simile of
concentrated waiting in ambush on the part of the robbers who
hold themselves in readiness to leap out and pounce upon the
victim is a reminder that our waiting upon the Lord in prayer
should be characterized by the same longing desire and eager
expectation. To translate the word *chākāh*, therefore, in Psalm
33:20, by the rather colorless "waiteth" tends to rob it of its
native verve and vigor. It need not connote a waiting upon God
in prayer that is vague, indifferent, purposeless, but a waiting that
is buoyant, resilient, eagerly expectant, as the context of Psalm
33:20 shows.

This is certainly where the emphasis lies in the Old Testament's use of the word. For example, the context of Isaiah 8:17
implies that the prophet anticipates a long period of waiting
upon the Lord. The people to whom he has been sent are indifferent. The Lord has hid His face from them. What, then,
is to be done in the circumstances? Isaiah binds up the testimony
he has already borne in Judah, seals up the teaching he has given,
commits it to the care of his disciples, and announces that he
and his disciples, and the Word of the Lord which he has proclaimed and committed to writing, will become signs in Judah;
and until there is a change of heart in the nation he will wait
upon the Lord, not in dumb resignation, however, but in faith,
as the words "and I will look for him" express. That this is
the look of egaer anticipation and not hopeless despair is clear
from Isaiah's use of *qāwāh* in 8:17, which the AV renders "look
for." To the man who waits upon God in this fashion, the future
is as bright as the promises of God, the hopelessness of the present
situation notwithstanding.

With this in mind, Isaiah 30:18 becomes doubly significant
because there the word *chākāh* is used with reference to the Lord's
waiting, as well as man's. The purpose of the Lord's waiting in
Isaiah 30:18 is twofold: "That he may be gracious unto you,"
and that He may be "exalted." But the former purpose pre-

dominates because the prophet emphasizes it by adding, "That he may have mercy upon you." Now the knowledge that God Himself waits, and the assurance that He waits only to show His grace and, through the manifesting of His grace, to be exalted among men, will lead praying people to wait upon the Lord in buoyant hope and resilient faith. Such a gracious God will finally respond to His waiting people in mercy; therefore Isaiah can add, "Blessed are all they that wait for him." In the inspiration of the same conviction the prophet exclaims, "We have waited . . . he will save . . . we will be glad and rejoice in his salvation" (25:9).

The same emphasis is found in Habakkuk's use of this word in 2:1-3. The prophet goes up to a lookout tower in order to stand upon his watch. As he keeps watch from the tower he "looks forth" (Heb. tsāphāh, to spy out, watch closely; from whence "Mizpah" in Gen. 31:49), both to hear what God has to say, and to see how he will answer the divine response. What God says is that Habakkuk's vision, seen from the lookout tower of prayer and communion will not be fulfilled immediately. He must, therefore, commit it to writing, but, "though it tarry, wait for it; because it will surely come." The moment of fulfillment is fixed, and against all appearances it is actually "hasting [Heb. pūach, panting] toward the end." Therefore, knowing that "it will surely come, it will not delay," there need be no fearful apprehension, as the people of God wait before Him in their lookout tower of prayer.

The same thought of waiting for the fulfillment of some word from the Lord is also present in Zephaniah 3:8, where the Lord commands the faithful, saying, "Wait ye for me . . . until the day that I rise up to the prey; for my determination is to gather the nations. . . ." A similar emphasis is found in Isaiah 64:4, a verse which is quoted by Paul in I Corinthians 2:9. Here the idea of earnest desire and ardent expectancy come shining through. The prophet's assurance is that "men have not heard, nor perceived by the ear, neither hath eye seen a God besides thee, who worketh"; but on whose behalf does this wonder-working God act? For those who wait for Him. A description of the people who thus wait expectantly follows in verses 5-12, of Isaiah 64. What mighty hope and faith, what eager expectation and largeness of petition, should break through all our waiting upon the Lord; especially as we purpose in our hearts to become pupils in Christ's school of prayer.

5. In the words already studied there has been a strong emphasis upon the individual aspect of our waiting upon the Lord. The remaining four words introduce the social view of prayer. This, it will be recalled, was strongly underlined in our Lord's teaching and practice of prayer. For example, the request by the Importunate Neighbor was on behalf of his friend; the use of the first person plural pronoun in the Lord's Prayer in Matthew 6 is another reminder; as is also the promise in Matthew 18:19, "If two of you shall agree . . . as touching anything," the ground of which is, "Where two or three are gathered together in my name, there am I in the midst" (v. 20). The next Hebrew word which we shall consider, therefore, is one that corresponds to the principle of *unity* in prayer, as laid down by Jesus in His teaching on the nature of prayer (pp. 20f.).

The word in question is *shāmar*. It means to watch, keep, observe, and is quite common in the Old Testament. It is this aspect of watching and observing that links *shāmar* with the subsidiary idea of waiting. For example, in Psalm 71:10 the psalmist complains that the people who take counsel together against him are lying in wait for him, but the word he uses is *shāmar*, to watch or observe. This sense of watching, which naturally involves "waiting in hiding," is frequent in the Old Testament (e.g., Judg. 1:24., Job 24:15, Ps. 56:6, Ps. 59, title). Of course, this watching and waiting could have a perfectly good sense as, for example, in Psalm 130:6, where the psalmist contrasts his waiting upon the Lord with the waiting of the watchman for the first flush of dawn. Now just as it was a sense of duty and unity that compelled the watchman to keep watch throughout the night, so it is the sense of unity with fellow Christians that compels us to keep in prayer.

The personal aspect of waiting in prayer in the sense of keeping watch is, of course, present in the Old Testament. It is found in Psalm 59:9 where, reading "my strength" (cf. v. 17) for "his strength," the psalmist determines to wait (Heb. "watch") before the Lord. Proverbs 8:34 is interesting. There personified Wisdom (cf. I Cor. 1:24, 30; Luke 11:49; Col. 2:3 with Prov. 8:12, 22, 23, 30), describes as blessed the man who waits (Heb. "watches") at the gate of Wisdom. The Greek rendering of Proverbs 8:34 uses a word which occurs only four times in the New Testament, and in three of these (Matt. 13:34, Luke 21:36, Eph. 6:18) the watching is linked indissolubly with prayer (see pp. 19f.). In the fourth instance, Hebrews 13:17, the strong probability is that the Church leaders who "watch in behalf of your souls, as they that shall give account," gave a large place to watching in prayer, in the discharge of their duties as overseers of the flock.

Now, just as the sense of unity between those who had oversight of the Church and the members of the Church led the former to watch and wait in prayer on behalf of those for whose spiritual welfare the Lord would hold them accountable, so in the case of those in the Old Testament who waited before the Lord in order to keep watch over others. There are three references where *shāmar*, to watch, has the sense of waiting in the place of devotion and worship; and they each concern the priests, and the discharge of their sacred duties in the tabernacle or temple, on behalf of the covenant community of Israel whom they represented before the Lord in the holy place. It is significant that Hebrew should use the word "to watch" to describe the priestly ministry of prayer. It was a reminder of the priest's indissoluble unity with the congregation of Israel.

One of the three references in question has no great significance for our purpose; it simply remarks that in Solomon's reign the organization of the priesthood had not been developed to the extent that the priests "waited by course," or regular rotation, on their ministry. The other two references are in Numbers. In 3:10 Moses is commanded to appoint Aaron and his sons to the priestly ministry to which God had called them. Here a dual unity is suggested: a unity among the priests themselves, and the unity that made them one with their lay brethren, whose representatives they were before God. In Numbers 3:10 the words "they shall keep [*shāmar*, watch or keep] their priesthood, are followed by the solemn warning, "the stranger that cometh nigh shall be put to death." Only members of the priestly tribe could participate in the priestly functions.

A similar warning occurs in Numbers 18:7, where the discharge of the priestly functions is again referred to in terms of watching or keeping the priesthood: the point of the warning, however, is not the same as in Numbers 3:10. No stranger is to come nigh to the place where the priestly functions were discharged because of the nature of these responsibilities. Since these included "everything of the altar within the veil," it would have been the most serious sacrilege for anyone to serve at the altar and within the veil who had not been ordained or appointed by God to that service.

The phrase, "and ye shall serve" (Numbers 18:7) means that the priest, in his waiting and watching in sacred things, was to consider that he was rendering a service; the thought being that at the altar and within the veil he was serving God, to whom the altar belonged, and man, on whose behalf he ministered in holy things. But the priest, appointed to this sacred service, was not to think that he was thereby superior to his lay brethren whom he represented at the altar (cf. p. 121). That is the force of the remark, "I give you the priesthood as a service of *gift*" (Num. 18:7). The priest had not attained his position through merit but by grace. All this is meaningful to those who, like the Twelve, say, "Lord, teach us to pray." Part of the answer to that request will include participation in the priestly ministry of intercession. The Biblical doctrine of the priesthood of all believers, based on our Lord's own High-Priestly ministry (pp. 120ff.), makes this possible, and the unity that binds all believers into one makes it necessary. Just how this works out in our prayer life today is partially disclosed by two other Hebrew words to which we must now turn our attention.

6. The sixth Hebrew word reminds us of yet another aspect of Christ's teaching concerning the nature of prayer — the necessity for *tenacity* in prayer (pp. 13ff.). This is the word *āmadh,* which means "to stand or stop," and is very common in the Old Testament. One reference will suffice to make plain its ordinary meaning. In I Kings 20:38 a prophet is said to have departed and waited for the king by the wayside. The word "waited" is the rendering of the Hebrew "to stand.'" The connection is fairly obvious. To stand waiting is a common idiom today; and it is used in the Old Testament with reference to waiting upon the Lord in prayer.

The word *āmadh,* to stand, is used in connection with the devotional life in many references, but it has the meaning of standing or waiting before the Lord in prayer only in three passages. In all three it has reference to the priestly ministry. It was understood that when the temple personnel stood to fulfill their mediatorial task they were waiting upon the Lord in prayer. In I Chronicles 6 the Levites who led the praise in public worship are described as having "waited on their office" in the house of the Lord (vv. 31-33). In II Chronicles 7 both the Levites, with their instruments of music, and the priests waited on their office (v. 6). The occasion was the dedication of the first temple. Again, in Nehemiah 12, the priests and the Levites wait in order to fulfill their ceremonial function. The office is the office of

God, the office imposed by, or due to, the Lord. The nature of this office upon which the temple personnel waited as they stood before God is explained in verses 44-45: "the charge [the ceremonial function] of purification." It was because the priests provided purification that "Judah rejoiced for the priests . . . that waited" ("stood," v. 44).

There are two other references that help us to fill out the meaning of these passages in Chronicles and Nehemiah. For example, the verb "to stand" (āmadh) is used in the Old Testament in the sense of presenting oneself before the Lord. In Deuteronomy 4:10 Israel stood before the Lord to enter into covenant with Him; in Deuteronomy 19:17, two men who had a controversy are required to appear (stand) before the Lord in the sanctuary to have their differences resolved; Jeremiah points out the futility of Judah standing, or presenting themselves, before the Lord while their unethical behavior condemns them (7:9-10); and in Leviticus 9, the congregation of Israel is commanded to draw near and stand before God when the sin-offering is being offered (v. 5).

The phrase is also used to denote that one is serving the Lord. Elijah uses it in the sense that he is the servant of the Lord (I Kings 17:1, 18:15); so also Elisha (II Kings 3:14, 5:16), and Jeremiah (15:19). Here the service is the fulfillment of the prophetic ministry. It may also denote the priestly ministry. What this means is plain from Deueronomy 10:8, where the priests not only bear the Ark of the Covenant, but also "stand before Jehovah to minister unto him, and to bless in his name." Phineas the priest stood before the Lord (Judg. 20:27-28), in order to find out, and then communicate, God's will for the people. Again, Ezekiel 44: 15-16 describes the priests standing before the Lord "to minister unto me; and to offer unto me the fat and the blood . . . and they shall come near to my table to minister unto me."

Men also stood before the Lord in order to intercede with Him on behalf of others. For example, in Genesis 18:22, Abraham stood before the Lord to intercede on behalf of Sodom. In Jeremiah 15:1 it is recalled how Moses (cf. Ex. 32:11-13), and Samuel (cf. I Sam. 7:9, 8:6, 12:23, 15:11) stood before the Lord to plead with God on behalf of others. And Jeremiah himself stood before the Lord to take part in this same ministry of intercession (18:20).

Now these references not only show what the Jews themselves would read into the ministry that the priests fulfilled as they stood waiting in the place of prayer, sacrifice, and worship, they also help us better to understand the significance of our own standing before God to wait upon Him in prayer. Applying the above references to our own prayer life, we stand to wait before God in prayer in order to enter into saving relations with Him through Christ, find the solution to the sinful divisions that separate us, serve the Lord and bless in His name, offer the sacrifice of praise, and intercede on behalf of others. Obviously all this is profoundly meaningful for us who are pupils in Christ's school of prayer.

7. It will have been realized that our study of the words *shāmar* (watch or observe), and *āmadh* (stand), as they are related to waiting upon God in prayer, has taken us away from what may be described as the passive aspect of our waiting before the Lord in prayer. Not only so, they have taken us out of the introspective or subjective sphere of prayer. The subjective aspect is inevitable in genuine prayer, but its dangers are obvious. We move even further away from this region when we consider the seventh Hebrew word, *tsābhā*. Here we are carried back to that part of Jesus' teaching on the nature of prayer that emphasizes *charity* (pp. 16f.). The word means "to wage war," "to go forth on military campaign." It is the root that gives the common word in the Old Testament for war, warfare, army, etc. It is also from this root that one of the most common titles given to the Lord is derived, that of *tsebhāōth*, meaning "host or armies." The full title is Jehovah God of Hosts, sometimes abbreviated to the Lord of Hosts. The title signified that the Lord was the God of battle, who marched at the head of the armies of Israel when they went forth to fight. It is this root, then, which has such strong military associations, that is used of the priestly waiting before God in the Old Testament.

In two instances, Exodus 38:8, I Samuel 2:22, the word signifies service, but it is not there applied to priests. It refers to duties performed by women in connection with the tabernacle. What those duties were is not at all clear, but in Exodus 38:8 "the ministering women that ministered" are said to have performed their services "at the door of the tent of meeting." In I Samuel 2:22 a period of spiritual declension in Israel witnesses the introduction of all kinds of moral irregularities where the serving women were concerned.

This idea of priestly service being understood in terms of spiritual warfare is found in several verses, and implies that priesthood in Israel involved the priests in charity toward their brethren. In Numbers 8:24, where reference to the Levites who were appointed to the work of the tent of meeting is made, we read, "They shall go in to wait upon the service in the work of the tent of meeting"; whereas the Hebrew reads, "They shall go in to war the warfare of the tent of meeting." At the age of fifty they were to retire from this service (v. 25). See also Numbers 4:23, and several other verses in this chapter (3, 30, 35, 39, 43) for the metaphorical use of the word warfare for the service done in the tabernacle.

In the Greek translation of the Old Testament a special word is used to describe this kind of service. It is the word *leitourgeō* and its cognates. Everywhere throughout the Septuagint this word is always used of the office or military service of priests and Levites, that is to say, of the religious service and religious ministration; that is to say, of service to God. A similar emphasis is found in the New Testament use of this word and its cognates. They refer to services rendered either to God or man, by apostles, prophets, teachers, and other officers of the Church.

The reference to Levitical service in the tabernacle in terms of military service, in Numbers 4 and 8, reminds us of Paul's affirmation that the Christian warfare is not against flesh and blood, but "against the spiritual hosts of wickedness in the heavenly places" (Eph. 6:10ff.). And it is significant that for Paul one of the most important weapons in the Christian soldier's armory, which he uses in this spiritual conflict, is prayer. The religious service, which is described as warfare in Numbers 4 and 8, was vicarious, in that it was waged on behalf of others; but whether it has reference to his own spiritual life, or to intercession for others, the Christian warrior who habitually waits upon God in prayer will find himself on the stretch for God as he participates in spiritual warfare in the secret place and will be reminded constantly of his need for a baptism into the love of God. Prayer is activity, it demands spiritual effort, it involves the Christian soldier's spirit in a tension similar to the tension that Jacob experienced on the banks of the Jabbok. All this is inevitable if a Christian importunes God to the extent that he refuses to let God go until prayer is answered. Those who determine to follow Christ's doctrine and practice of prayer engage themselves to fight the good fight of faith.

8. Thus far in our study of the Hebrew words rendered "wait on the Lord" in the Old Testament, both the individual and social aspects of prayer have been emphasized, but only in separation the one from the other. This final word expresses something that is common both to personal and corporate prayer. If

either, or both, are to be efficacious, expectancy must be supreme, an expectancy that is the outreaching of the hand of faith; and since *expectancy* is of the essence of prayer, as Jesus' teaching on prayer makes clear (pp. 21f.), this last of the eight Hebrew words we are studying provides yet another point of contact between the Old and the New Testaments; or more specifically, we reach yet another point where the Old Testament is mirrored in the teaching of our Lord.

The Hebrew word that communicates the element of expectancy and eager anticipation to our waiting upon God in prayer is *yāchal*. Its basic meaning is to wait or tarry, as is seen in its use by Samuel when he commanded Saul to precede him to Gilgal, saying, "Seven days shalt thou *tarry*, till I come unto thee" (I Sam. 10:8, cf. also 8:8). The Greek of the Septuagint here has *dialeipō*, which occurs only once in the New Testament, Luke 7:45, where it is used negatively, and means "to intermit," "leave off for a time."

To the ordinary meaning of waiting is added the idea of expectancy in Job's use of *yāchal* in 30:26, where he "waited for light," but the eager anticipation was disappointed because instead of light "there came darkness." Another very interesting use of the word occurs in Genesis 8:10, 12. In verse 10, where *yāchal* should be read, Noah, after receiving the dove into the ark on the first occasion, "stayed yet another seven days"; and so similarly on the second return of the dove to the ark in verse 12. The use of *yāchal* here, which conveys the idea of waiting expectantly, suggests that Noah's was not the waiting of blank despair but of unshakable hope, the conviction that God would deliver completely. The Septuagint word in these two verses in Genesis 8 and in Job 30:26 occurs in Luke 14:7, where our Lord was "remarking" (AV) how the guests chose the seats of honor at the feasts: that is to say, Jesus was waiting to see what they would do in expectation that they would act in the manner which He had already anticipated.

This thought is even clearer from Acts 3:5 where the same Greek word occurs. There the beggar at the gate Beautiful, to whom Peter and John said, "look on us," in response to the command "gave heed unto them"; that is to say, waited, but with eager anticipation; an expectation which Luke actually expresses when he remarks that the beggar was "expecting to receive something from them." Notice, too, Acts 19:22, where Paul's staying on in Asia, after Timothy and Erastus left him, is described, not by the usual word to wait or tarry in the sense of hanging about idly and aimlessly, but by the word that expresses waiting with eager hope and assured expectancy, believing that God would do mighty things through Paul. For the fulfillment of Paul's expectation, kept alive while he waited, see the remainder of Acts 19. The use by Paul of this same word in Philippians 2:16, where it is rendered "holding forth [i. e., offering] the word of life," indicates that for him the preaching of the gospel must be characterized by eager expectancy and anticipation, as the preacher of the Word waits for results to follow the proclamation.

Now all this illustrates what the Hebrew word *yāchal* conveys, when used in the Old Testament with reference to our waiting upon God in prayer. It suggests that in all our waiting upon the Lord our spirits should be liberated from the hopelessness and listlessness of despair that inhibits faith in God, and so frustrates prayer that it is robbed of its vitality and reality. Unfortunately, our waiting upon God is so dogged by despondency that we betray ourselves into crying with king Ahab, "Behold, this trouble is from the Lord; why should I wait (*yāchal*) for the Lord any longer?" How familiar is that sentiment! The "trouble" was a three years' famine, and ironically enough Ahab's petulant outburst was met with the assurance that flour would be sold in the gate of Samaria the very next day! (II Kings 6:33, 7:1). In spite of apparent divine carelessness or indifference our waiting upon the Lord must ever be instinct with hope; not the hope of dumb resignation but of unwavering, informed faith in God. This is well expressed in Psalm 69:3 where in spite of general weariness and hoarseness of throat and failing eyes due to his agonized crying during prolonged waiting before God, the psalmist waits on in undying hope, a hope that blossoms forth into a great faith that God will yet hear his prayer (vv. 30-36). See also Psalm 130; 31:24, 33:18, 38:15, where "hope" is rendered "wait" in the margin.

This persistence in waiting in hope, and, like Abraham, believing against hope (Rom. 4:18) in a situation that appears to be hopeless, is nowhere more strongly expressed than in Lamentations 3. It is, of course, Jerusalem, sacked and desolated by the Babylonians when they captured it in 586 B.C., who is soliloquizing in verse 18. She says to herself, "My strength is perished, and mine expectation (*yāchal*) from Jehovah." Then, in the midst of her desolating misery she begins to reflect. Memory gets to work; and as she remembrs the past she murmurs in verse 21, "This I recall

to my mind, therefore have I hope" (*yāchal*). And as the almost
extinguished flame of hope begins to burn within Jerusalem's
breast, in spite of the hopelessness of her present situation she
recalls, "Jehovah is my portion . . . therefore will I hope (*yāchal*)
in him." And now, with hope reviving, she affirms, "It is good
that a man should hope (*yāchal*) and quietly wait for the salvation of Jehovah" (v. 26). Similar soliloquizing is found in
Psalm 42:5, 11, 43:5, where the psalmist, in spite of being downcast in soul, and disquieted within, determines to hope in God,
believing that he shall yet have good cause to praise God.

In the light of these reflections we are now better able to ap-
preciate just how insipid this great word *yāchal* can appear to be
when it is rendered by the rather colorless word "wait" in the
AV. Micah 7:7 is perhaps as good an illustration of this as can
be found in the Old Testament. "Therefore I will look unto the
Lord; I will wait for the God of my salvation: my God will hear
me," is the AV rendering of the Hebrew. There are three things
to notice here.

(i) That the waiting for the Lord in this verse is the waiting
in prayer, is clear from the last clause, "He will hear me." (ii)
That looking unto the Lord is no ordinary exercise, is clear from
the word Micah uses. It is *tsāphāh*, which Habakkuk uses in
2:1 of his looking forth from his watchtower. In Genesis 39:41 it
refers to the Lord's watching between Laban and Jacob to see
that neither broke the covenant bond. Elsewhere it refers to the
Lord's keeping watch upon the nations (Ps. 66:9), of the watchman (II Sam. 13:34), and in this sense figuratively of the prophets (Jer. 6:17, Ezek. 3:17, 33:7, Isa. 52:8, 56:10). In Micah 7:7,
where the prophet refers to the relation between his public ministry and his prayer life, he will keep watch in the expectation that
he will see in reality what he at the moment waits and watches
for in faith. (iii) As Micah watches, he waits for the God of
his salvation; and his is the waiting of undying hope and uncon-
querable faith that will trust and not be afraid, no matter how
foreboding the circumstances may be in which he waits (*yāchal*)
for the God of his salvation. It is in the same unshakable assurance that the coastlands wait for Messiah, and for Messiah's
law (Isa. 42:4, 51:5).

The sum of the matter, then, is this: these eight words, taken
singly or together, point to what the most spiritual in ancient
Israel meant when they spoke of waiting upon God in prayer. It
included silence (*dūm*), the silence of *humility;* and it included

waiting (*chākāh*) in its *simplicity*. This exercise of the spirit imposed a searching discipline upon those who thus waited, a discipline that was understood in terms of *intensity* (*qāwāh*) because the waiting in prayer involved *importunity* (*chūl*). There was, then, no room for complacency or smugness or morbid self-interest. This was waiting upon God that was watching (*shāmar*), because the one who waited in prayer realized his *unity* with his brother Israelites. His waiting upon God meant that he stood (*āmadh*) before the Lord with *tenacity;* and while he stood before God his heart went out in *charity* towards his brethren on whose behalf he waged the warfare (*tsābhā*) of prayer in the secret place; not despondently but in hope (*yāchal*), and dauntless *expectancy*.

As already suggested, all this is powerfully reminiscent of our Lord's own prayer life as depicted in the Gospels, and of His teaching on prayer. These characteristics of the prayer life in ancient Israel, which are reflected in the Old Testament, were the constitutive elements in Christ's own prayers, only, in His experience they found their purest and profoundest expression. And in reply to those who appeal to Him to teach them how to pray He points to His own prayer life, saying, "Follow me." In the indwelling presence of the Holy Spirit there is adequate spiritual dynamic to enable every Christian to respond to this invitation. As each responds he will find that in the measure in which he desires that Christ should teach him how to pray, the Spirit will help him in his infirmities, and will make intercession, intercession which, although expressed in sighs too deep for words, is understood, and fulfilled, by God the Father. And if that is not assurance enough, Christ Himself will also intercede for every Christian who desires to learn to pray in the Master's school of prayer.

BIBLIOGRAPHY

CHAPTER ONE

Alford, Henry: *The Greek Testament,* Vol. I, New York: Harper, 1859

Bruce, A. B.: *The Synoptic Gospels (The Expositor's Greek Testament)*, Grand Rapids: reprinted by Eerdmans

Bruce, A. B.: *The Training of the Twelve,* New York: 1891

Catholic Commentary on Holy Scripture, A, New York: Nelson, 1953

Dods, Marcus: *The Gospel of St. John (The Expositor's Greek Testament)*, Grand Rapids: reprinted by Eerdmans

Dummelow, J. R.: *A Commentary on the Holy Bible,* New York: Macmillan, 1909

Gore, Goudge, Guillaume: *A New Commentary on Holy Scripture,* New York: Macmillan, 1929

Gould, E. P.: *The Gospel According to St. Mark (The International Critical Commentary)*, New York: Scribner's, 1896

Hastings, James: *A Dictionary of the Bible,* New York: Scribner's, 1902; article on Prayer

Hastings, James: *Dictionary of Christ and the Gospels,* New York: Scribner's, 1917; articles on Prayer and Intercession

Horton, R. F.: *A Devotional Commentary on St. Matthew,* New York: Revell, 1907

Micklem, P. A.: *The Gospel According to St. Matthew (Westminster Commentaries)*, London: Methuen, 1917

Plummer, A.: *An Exegetical Commentary on the Gospel According to St. Matthew,* Grand Rapids: reprinted by Eerdmans

Plummer, A.: *St. Mark (Cambridge Greek Testament)*, Cambridge: The University Press, 1938

Plummer, A.: *St. John (Cambridge Greek Testament)*, Cambridge: The University Press, 1912

Strachan, R. H.: *The Fourth Gospel,* London: Student Christian Movement Press, 1911

Westcott, B. F.: *The Gospel According to St. John,* Grand Rapids: reprinted by Eerdmans

CHAPTER TWO

Similar to those listed under Chapter One.

CHAPTER THREE

Alford, Henry: *The Greek Testament,* Vol. I, New York: Harper, 1959

Catholic Commentary on Holy Scripture, A, New York: Nelson, 1953

Dods, Marcus: *The Gospel of St. John* (*The Expositor's Greek Testament*), Grand Rapids: reprinted by Eerdmans

Dummelow, J. R.: *A Commentary on the Holy Bible,* New York: Macmillan, 1909

Gore, Goudge, Guillaume: *A Commentary on Holy Scripture,* New York: Macmillan, 1929

Plummer, A.: *St. John* (*Cambridge Greek Testament*), Cambridge: The University Press, 1912

Robertson, A. T.: *Word Pictures in the New Testament,* Vol. V, Nashville, Tennessee: Sunday School Board of the Southern Baptist Convention, 1932

Strachan, R. H.: *The Fourth Gospel,* London: Student Christian Movement Press, 1941

Swete, H. B.: *The Last Discourse and Prayer of Our Lord,* London: Macmillan, 1913

Temple, William: *Readings in St. John's Gospel,* London: Macmillan, 1952

Westcott, B. F.: *The Gospel According to St. John,* Grand Rapids: reprinted by Eerdmans

CHAPTER FOUR

Alford, Henry: *The Greek Testament,* Vol. I, New York: Harper, 1859

Bruce, A. B.: *The Synoptic Gospels* (*The Expositor's Greek Testament*), Grand Rapids: reprinted by Eerdmans

Calvin, John: *Institutes,* translated by H. Beveridge, Vol. II, Bk. III, Chap. XX, Grand Rapids: reprinted by Eerdmans

Catholic Commentary on Holy Scripture, A, New York: Nelson 1953

Dummelow, J. R.: *A Commentary on the Holy Bible*, New York: Macmillan, 1909

Godet, F.: *A Commentary on the Gospel of St. Luke*, Grand Rapids: reprinted by Zondervan

Gore, Goudge, Guillaume: *A Commentary on Holy Scripture*, New York: Macmillan, 1929

Hastings, James: *A Dictionary of the Bible*, New York: Scribner's, 1902; article on Lord's Prayer

Hastings, James: *A Dictionary of Christ and the Gospels*, New York: Scribner's, 1917; article on the Lord's Prayer

Horton, R. F.: *A Devotional Commentary on St. Matthew*, New York: Revell, 1907

Micklem, P. A.: *The Gospel According to St. Matthew (Westminster Commentaries)*, London: Methuen, 1917

Plummer, A.: *An Exegetical Commentary on the Gospel According to St. Matthew*, Grand Rapids: reprinted by Eerdmans

CHAPTER FIVE

Alford, Henry: *The Greek Testament*, Vol. IV, London: Rivington's, 1861

Davidson, A. B.: *Hebrews (Hand-Books for Bible Classes)*, Edinburgh: T. & T. Clark

Denny, James: *Studies in Theology*, Lecture VII, New York: Armstrong, 1901

Dods, Marcus: *The Epistle to the Hebrews (The Expositor's Greek Testament)*, Grand Rapids: reprinted by Eerdmans

Farrar, F. W.: *Hebrews (Cambridge Greek Testament)*, Cambridge: The University Press, 1894

Hastings, James: *A Dictionary of the Bible*, New York: Scribner's, 1902; article on Priest in the New Testament

Hastings, James: *Dictionary of Christ and the Gospels*, New York: Scribner's, 1917; articles on Priest and Mediator

Hastings, James: *Dictionary of the Apostolic Church*, New York: Scribner's; article on Priest